A. Lincoln

LINCOLN'S OWN STORIES

COLLECTED AND EDITED BY
ANTHONY GROSS

WITH PORTRAIT

HARPER & BROTHERS PUBLISHERS
NEW YORK AND LONDON

COPYRIGHT, 1912, BY HARPER & BROTHERS

PRINTED IN THE UNITED STATES OF AMERICA
PUBLISHED OCTOBER, 1912

**AFFECTIONATELY DEDICATED
TO MY BROTHER
SYDNEY**

CONTENTS

PART		PAGE
	Introduction	v
I.	Earlier Years	1
II.	The Lawyer	13
III.	Local Politics and the Douglas Debates	45
IV.	At the White House	67
V.	At the Front	135
VI.	The Commander-in-Chief	159

INTRODUCTION

FOR many years the editor has collected and studied the literature relating to Abraham Lincoln, and his interest has led to the preparation of a book which he has endeavored to make both authentic and significant. His purpose has been to select stories which embody truth and point, and to arrange them, as far as possible, consecutively, so that they may furnish continuous illustrations of the various stages of Lincoln's wonderful career. Various dubious and often maudlin tales which have been attributed to Lincoln have been omitted. While it would be impossible to claim that any collection is absolutely comprehensive, yet it is believed that the best and the essential Lincoln stories are assembled here in a manner which will serve as an outline biography in story form.

In connection with this plan the bare facts of Lincoln's life may be restated helpfully. His parents, born in Virginia, followed the westward

INTRODUCTION

movement across the Alleghanies to Kentucky, where Abraham Lincoln was born in Hardin County on February 12, 1809. Afterward the family continued westward to Indiana. His education, acquired almost entirely by himself, included hardly more than a year at a regular school. His was the working boyhood of the frontier. At nineteen he helped to take a flatboat down the Mississippi to New Orleans, and the fidelity of his service caused his employer to make him a clerk and to give him charge of a store at New Salem, Illinois. In 1832 the force of Lincoln's personality led to his election as captain of a company raised for the Black Hawk War. Next came his appointment as postmaster at New Salem, his study of law, and his admission, in 1836, to the practice of law, which he began at Springfield, Illinois. Law almost inevitably involved politics, and Lincoln's growing success as a lawyer was accompanied by recognition as a locally conspicuous figure in the Whig party. There followed, naturally, various elections to the Legislature, and finally, in 1847, his election to Congress, where he emphasized his antagonism to slavery. His selection as a candidate for the Senate of the United States, in 1858, led to the historic debates with Stephen A. Douglas. Lincoln obtained the popular vote,

INTRODUCTION

but the Legislature elected Douglas. Yet the real outcome was a national prominence which brought him the Republican nomination for the Presidency over William H. Seward, in 1860, and his election. So far as possible Lincoln's great career as President has been divided into three parts which afford stories of the civil side of his administration, stories of his visits to the front, and stories relating peculiarly to the events of the war. Obviously the line cannot be drawn sharply; but the general plan will, it is believed, be found convenient as affording illuminating suggestions regarding the various phases of the momentous period from Lincoln's first election to his death, April 15, 1865.

Abraham Lincoln was a man of steel nerves, clear mental grasp, stanch convictions, and adamantine will, though withal a man of the gentlest and kindliest character; and his forbearance and patience were almost infinite. He was the genius of common sense. His steps forward were always well timed, and some one said that he was never oppressed with that curse of genius, the self-consciousness of petty things. He had the faculty of picking out the essentials of a question and allowing the non-essentials to take care of themselves.

His stories illustrate these characteristics to a

INTRODUCTION

marked degree. They were told for a purpose. He was not a professional story-teller. That is, he did not tell stories for the sake of exploiting his humor. He told them as they were called into being by events; sometimes to illumine an argument or to controvert one; very often to conceal his purposes or to throw some persistent inquirer off the trail; at times to let down an ardent office-seeker gently. But he was a man of infinite jest in the most human sense, and if this modest compilation serves to accentuate his kindliness and patience, his tactfulness and sagacity, his great patriotism and wisdom, his unselfish devotion to the highest ideals, it will help to a closer understanding of one of the great characters of the world's unfolding drama.

My thanks are due to the many lovers and biographers of Lincoln, to authors of standard books, and to various chroniclers, from whom these stories have been gathered.

Part I
EARLIER YEARS

LINCOLN'S OWN STORIES

I

EARLIER YEARS

WHEN the Lincoln family moved from Indiana to Illinois in the spring of 1830 they had, among their few possessions, a small pet dog. The little animal fell behind one day and was not missed until the party had crossed a swollen, ice-filled stream, when he made his presence on the opposite bank known by whines and yelps. Lincoln's father, anxious to go forward, decided not to recross the river with oxen and wagons, but the boy Abraham could not endure the idea of abandoning even a dog. Pulling off shoes and socks, he waded across the stream and triumphantly returned with the shivering animal under his arm. Said Lincoln afterward, "His frantic leaps of joy and other evidences of a dog's gratitude amply repaid me for all the exposure I had undergone."

LINCOLN'S OWN STORIES

In his youth Lincoln ran a ferry in the Ohio River at the mouth of Anderson Creek. The only passenger for a whole day was being ferried over, and to enliven the journey he told the story of Washington throwing a silver dollar across the Rappahannock at Fredericksburg.

"Well," remarked young Abraham, sadly, "he couldn't throw one across the Ohio at the mouth of Anderson unless he was doing more business than I am, or unless he stole it."

When Lincoln came on a visit to his father's home in Coles County, Illinois, in 1831, his reputation as a great wrestler had preceded him. The local champion, one Daniel Needham, promptly challenged him, and Lincoln promptly accepted. In the public contest which followed Lincoln threw his opponent twice with comparative ease and thus aroused the anger of Needham.

"Lincoln," he shouted, "you have thrown me twice, but you can't whip me!"

"Needham," he answered, "are you satisfied that I can throw you? If you are not, and must be convinced by a thrashing, I will do that, too, for your sake."

In 1832, at the time of the Black Hawk War, Lincoln was drilling his men, and they were marching with twenty men fronting in line across a field when he wished to pass through a gate into the next field. "I could not for the life of me," said Lincoln, "remember the proper word of command for getting my company 'endwise,' so that it could get through the gate, so, as we came near the gate, I shouted: 'This company is dismissed for two minutes, when it will fall in again on the other side of the gate.'"

Lincoln had great moral courage, which is shown in the following letter, certainly an excellent one for a twenty-seven-year-old backwoodsman:

"NEW SALEM, *June 21, 1836.*

"DEAR COLONEL,—I am told that during my absence last week you passed through the place and stated publicly that you were in possession of a fact or facts which, if known to the public, would entirely destroy the prospects of N. W. Edwards and myself at the coming election, but that through favor to us you would forbear to divulge them. No one has needed favors more than I, and few, generally, have been less unwilling to accept them; but in this case favor to me would be injustice to the public, and therefore I must beg your pardon for declining it.

That I once had the confidence of the people

of Sangamon County is sufficiently evident; and if I have done anything, either by design or misadventure, which if known would subject me to a forfeiture of that confidence, he that knows of that thing and conceals it is a traitor to his country's interest.

"I find myself wholly unable to form any conjecture of what fact or facts, real or supposed, you spoke; but my opinion of your veracity will not permit me for a moment to doubt that you at least believed what you said. I am flattered with the personal regard you manifested for me; but I do hope that, on mature reflection, you will view the public interest as a paramount consideration and therefore determine to let the worst come.

"I assure you that the candid statement of facts on your part, however low it may sink me, shall never break the ties of personal friendship between us.

"I wish an answer to this, and you are at liberty to publish both if you choose.

"Very respectfully,
"A. LINCOLN.
"COL. ROBERT ALLEN."

His retort to a Democratic demagogue, one Col. Dick Taylor, is famous. Taylor charged

EARLIER YEARS

Lincoln and his friends with being "rag-barons and manufacturing lords." "To take the wind out of his sails," as Lincoln aptly put it, he slipped up to the speaker's side and gave his vest a sharp pull. "It displayed to the astonished audience a mass of ruffled shirt, gold watch, chains, seals, and glittering jewels," says a narrator. Lincoln in his rough clothes and coarse linen was quick to take advantage of this unusual display of finery.

"Behold the hard-fisted Democrat! Look, gentlemen, at this specimen of the bone and sinew. And here, gentlemen," laying his coarse hand on his heart and bowing, "here at your service, here is your aristocrat! Here is one of your silk-stockinged gentry. Here is your rag-baron with his lily-white hands. Yes, I suppose I, according to my friend Taylor, am a bloated aristocrat.

"While Colonel Taylor was making his charges against the Whigs over the country, riding in fine carriages, wearing ruffled shirts, kid gloves, massive gold watch-chains with large gold seals, and flourishing a gold-headed cane, I was a poor boy, hired on a flatboat at eight dollars a month, and had only one pair of breeches to my back, and they buckskin. Now, if you know the nature of buckskin, when wet and dried by the sun it will shrink, and my breeches kept shrinking until they left several inches of my legs bare, between the tops of my socks and the lower part of my breeches; and while I was growing taller they were becoming shorter, and so much tighter that they left a blue streak around my legs that can be seen to this day. If you call this aristocracy, I plead guilty to the charge."

Thus did he pillory this demagogue.

Lincoln had great physical courage, also. Once his friend Edward Baker, famous for his impetuous eloquence, attacked a local newspaper before an audience of voters. It took place immediately beneath the office of Stuart & Lincoln. Lincoln lay listening through a trap door that separated the two floors.

"Pull him down," shouted the brother of the newspaper editor, and for a moment it looked rather ominous for Baker. The crowd advanced, when to his astonishment the lank form of Lincoln dangled to the platform below. Gesticulating in vain for silence, he seized the stone water-jug and shouted:

"I'll break it over the head of the first man who lays a hand on Baker!" And then he continued:

"Hold on, gentlemen, let us not disgrace the

EARLIER YEARS

age and country in which we live. This is a land where freedom of speech is guaranteed. Mr. Baker has a right to speak and ought to be permitted to do so. I am here to protect him, and no man shall take him from this stand if I can prevent him." And order was restored.

Another instance may be here recited. General Usher F. Linder delivered a rather spirited address amid threats of violence from the galleries. Lincoln and Baker got on the platform and stationed themselves beside the speaker. When he had finished Lincoln said:

"Linder, Baker and I are apprehensive that you may be attacked by some of those ruffians who insulted you from the galleries, and we have come to escort you to your hotel. We both think we can do a little fighting, so we want you to walk between us until we get you to your hotel. Your quarrel is our quarrel and that of the great Whig party of this nation; and your speech upon this occasion is the greatest one that has been made by any of us, for which we wish to honor, love, and defend you." And they walked off unmolested, amid the cheers of the audience.

These were rough days and violence often extended to the polls. A railroad contractor named Radford had taken possession of a polling-place during the "hard-cider campaign" and prevented the Whigs from voting. Lincoln seized an ax-handle and made for the place.

"Radford," he said, "you'll spoil and blow if you live much longer."

Knowing the character of Lincoln, Radford discreetly retired, to the disappointment of the candidate, who told Speed that he wanted Radford to show fight, as he "intended just to knock him down and leave him kicking."

His power of invective and ridicule is exemplified in the remarkable "Rebecca" letters. Speaking of Shields, then the Auditor of the State and a very prominent Democratic politician, Lincoln wrote in the local paper, in a humorous burlesque style:

"I seed him when I was down in Springfield last winter. They had a sort of gatherin' there one night among the grandees; they called it a fair. All the gals about town was there, and all the handsome widows and married women, finickin' about trying to look like gals. . . . I looked in at the window, and there this same fellow Shields floatin' about on the air, without heft or earthly substances, just like a lock of cat fur where cats had been fighting. He was paying his money to this one and that one and t'other one, and sufferin' great loss because it wasn't silver instead of State paper; and the sweet distress he seemed to be in—his very features, in the ecstatic agony of his soul, spoke audibly and distinctly: 'Dear girls, it is most distressing, but I cannot marry you all. Too well I know how much you suffer; but do, do remember, it is not my fault that I am so handsome and interesting.' As this last was expressed by a most exquisite contortion of his face, he seized hold of one of their hands and squeezed and held on to it about a quarter of an hour. 'Oh, my good fellow!' says I to myself, 'if that was one of our Democratic gals in the Lost Townships, the way you'd get a brass pin let into you would be about up to the head.'"

This is very witty, but Lincoln could be very severe and at times, or rather at that time, abusive, as his answer to a circular issued by Auditor Shields shows:

"I say it's a lie, and not a well-told one at that. It grins out like a copper dollar. Shields is a fool as well as a liar. With him truth is out of the question, and as for getting a good, bright, passable lie out of him, you might as well try to strike fire from a cake of tallow."

Strong words these, which very nearly led to a duel.

LINCOLN'S OWN STORIES

Something was once said about the wild-cat Western currency of seventy years ago, a species of paper money then worth about as much as Confederate bills were worth after Lee's surrender (at the latter time a parcel containing over a thousand dollars was offered for five dollars). Mr. Lincoln's story was that he was going down the Mississippi. Fuel was getting low and the captain directed the pilot to steer in to the first woodpile that he saw on the river-bank. When the captain reached one he said to the owner on shore, "Is that your wood?" "Certainly." "You want to sell it?" "Yes." "Will you accept currency?" "Certainly." "How will you take it?" said the captain; to which the owner promptly replied: "Cord for cord."

His great tenderness in love and sorrow is shown when Anne Rutledge, his first love, was laid in the grave. Grieving till his friends feared his loss of reason, he was found on a dark and stormy night beside the new-made grave crying, "I cannot bear to have the rain fall upon her."

Speaking of his ancestry, Lincoln once humorously remarked, "I don't know who my grandfather was, and I am much more concerned to know what his grandson will be."

Part II
THE LAWYER

II

THE LAWYER

LINCOLN'S family devotion was unbounded and he loved his children to the verge of folly. He delighted to carry his boys on his back and to take one of them by the hand when he went to town. Their turmoil never disturbed him. Their mischief only amused him; he never viewed it with alarm. "Since I began this letter," he wrote to a friend, "a messenger came to tell me that Bob was lost; but by the time I reached the house his mother had found him and had him whipped, and by now, very likely, he is run away again."

When this same Bob was bitten by a dog, his anxious and always superstitious father dropped everything and took him to Indiana, that a wonderful madstone in that State might be applied to the wound.

The boys could go to Lincoln's law office and pull down the law-books, scatter legal documents over the floor, and bend the points of the pens without ruffling his temper, however much they annoyed his partner.

Here is a rather curious illustration of Lincoln's humor, and likewise his exalted and unusual honesty. In a letter to the proprietors of a wholesale store in Louisville, for whom suit had been brought, after notifying his client of the sale of certain real estate in satisfaction of their judgment, he adds: "As to the real estate, we cannot attend to it. We are not real estate agents, we are lawyers. We recommend that you give the charge of it to Mr. Isaac S. Britton, a trustworthy man, and one whom the Lord made on purpose for such business."

Returning at one time from the circuit he said to his law-partner, Mr. Herndon: "Billy, I heard a good story while I was up in the country. Judge D—— was complimenting the landlord on the excellency of his beef. 'I am surprised,' he said, 'that you have such good beef; you must have to kill a whole critter when you want any.' 'Yes,' said the landlord, 'we never kill less than a whole critter.'"

Mr. Lincoln was once engaged in the trial of a suit involving the infringement of a patent

THE LAWYER

water-wheel. In his earlier days he had aided in running a sawmill, and he explained in his argument, in a very clear and masterly manner, all the intricate points involved in the action of the water. After the jury retired he became quite anxious and uneasy. The jury were in another building, the windows of which opened on the street, and they had been out about two hours. As Lincoln was passing along the street one of the jurors, on whom he very much relied, as he was a very intelligent man and firm in his convictions, looked out of the window and held up one finger. Mr. Lincoln became very much excited, fearing that it indicated eleven of the jury against him. He knew that if this man was for him he never would yield his opinion, and added that it reminded him very much of another case in which he was involved, and if the two jurors were alike in their action his client was safe. He said that he had been employed to prosecute a suit for divorce. His client was a pretty, refined, and interesting little woman who was in court. The defendant, her husband, was a gross, morose, and uncomfortable man; but although Lincoln was able to prove the use of very offensive and vulgar epithets applied by the husband to his wife, and all sorts of annoyances, yet there were no such acts of personal violence as were required by the statutes to justify divorce. Lincoln did the best he could and appealed to the jury to have compassion for the woman and not to bind her to such a man and such a life as awaited her if required to live longer with him. The jury took about the same view of it in their deliberations. They were anxious to find for the woman, but there was no evidence to justify such a verdict. At last they drew up a verdict for the defendant and all signed but one fellow, who, on being approached, coolly said, "Gentlemen, I am going to lie down to sleep, and when you get ready to give a verdict for that little woman then wake me up and not until then; for before I will give a verdict against her I will lie here till I rot and the pismires carry me out through the keyhole." "Now," observed Mr. Lincoln, "if that juryman would stick like the other fellow, we are safe." Strange to relate, the jury did come in and bring a verdict for the defendant.

Here's a rather homely way in which Lincoln once described the manner in which his memory worked. It was once said to him that his mind was a wonderful one; that impressions were easily made upon it and never effaced. "No," said he, "you are mistaken; I am slow to learn

THE LAWYER

and slow to forget that which I have learned. My mind is like a piece of steel—very hard to scratch anything on it, and almost impossible, after you get it there, to rub it out."

George W. Miner tells the following story of the manner in which Mr. Lincoln handled a jury: "In the spring term of the Tazewell County Court, in 1847, I was detained as a witness. Lincoln was employed in several suits, and among them was one of Case vs. Snow Brothers. The Snow Brothers (who were both minors) had purchased from a Mr. Case what was then called a 'prairie team,' consisting of two or three yoke of oxen and a prairie plow, giving therefor their joint note for some two hundred dollars; but when pay-day came they refused to pay, pleading the minor act. The note was placed in Lincoln's hands for collection. The suit was called and a jury impaneled. The Snow Brothers did not deny the note, but pleaded through their counsel that they were minors, and that Mr. Case knew they were at the time of the contract and conveyance. All this was admitted by Mr. Lincoln, with his peculiar phrase, 'Yes, gentlemen, I reckon that's so.' The minor act was read and its validity admitted in the same manner. The counsel for the defendants were permitted without question

LINCOLN'S OWN STORIES

to state all these things to the jury, and to show by the statute that these minors could not be held responsible for their contract. By this time you may well suppose that his client became quite uneasy. 'What!' thought I, 'this good old man who confided in these boys to be wronged in this way, and even his counsel, Mr. Lincoln, to submit in silence.' I looked at Judge Treat, but could read nothing in his calm and dignified demeanor. Just then Mr. Lincoln slowly rose to his strange, half-erect attitude and in clear, quiet accents began: 'Gentlemen of the jury, are you willing to allow these boys to begin life with this shame and disgrace attached to their character? If you are, I am not. The best judge of human character that ever wrote has left these immortal words for us to ponder:

"Good name in man or woman, dear my lord,
Is the immediate jewel of their souls:
Who steals my purse steals trash; 'tis something, nothing;
'Twas mine, 'tis his, and has been slave to thousands;
But he that filches from me my good name
Robs me of that which not enriches him
And makes me poor indeed.

"Then rising to his full height, and looking upon the defendants with the compassion of a brother,

THE LAWYER

his long arm extended toward the opposing counsel, he continued: 'Gentlemen of the jury, these poor innocent boys would never have attempted this low villainy had it not been for the advice of these lawyers.' Then for a few minutes he showed how even the noble science of law may be prostituted. With a scathing rebuke to those who thus belittle their profession, he concluded: 'And now, gentlemen, you have it in *your* power to set these boys right before the world.' He pleaded for the young men only; I think he did not mention his client's name. The jury, without leaving their seats, decided that the defendants must pay the debt; and the latter, after hearing Lincoln, were as willing to pay it as the jury were determined they should. I think the entire argument lasted not above five minutes."

To a man who once offered him a case the merits of which he did not appreciate he made, according to his partner, Mr. Herndon, the following response:

"Yes, there is no reasonable doubt that I can gain your case for you. I can set a whole neighborhood at loggerheads; I can distress a widowed mother and her six fatherless children, and thereby get for you six hundred dollars which rightly belong, it appears to me, as much to them as it does to you. I shall not take your case, but I will give you a little advice for nothing. You seem a sprightly, energetic man. I would advise you to try your hand at making six hundred dollars in some other way."

Once he was prosecuting a civil suit, in the course of which evidence was introduced showing that his client was attempting a fraud. Lincoln rose and went to his hotel in deep disgust. The judge sent for him; he refused to come. "Tell the judge," he said, "my hands are dirty; I came over to wash them."

At another time, when he was engaged with Judge S. C. Parks in defending a man accused of larceny, he said, "If you can say anything for the man, do it—I can't; if I attempt it, the jury will see I think he is guilty, and convict him."

This is from Chauncey M. Depew: "President Lincoln told me once that, in his judgment, one of the two best things he ever originated was this. He was trying a case in Illinois where he appeared for a prisoner charged with aggravated assault and battery. The complainant had told a horrible story of the attack, which his appearance fully justified, when the district-attorney handed the witness over to Mr. Lincoln for cross-examination. Mr. Lincoln said he had no testimony, and unless he could break down the complainant's story he saw no way out. He had come to the conclusion that the witness was a bumptious man, who rather prided himself upon his smartness in repartee, and so, after looking at him for some minutes, he inquired, 'Well, my friend, what ground did you and my client here fight over?' The fellow answered, 'About six acres.' 'Well,' said Mr. Lincoln, 'don't you think this is an almighty small crop of fight to gather from such a big piece of ground?' The jury laughed, the court and district-attorney and complainant all joined in, and the case was laughed out of court."

Leonard Swett, of Chicago, for years an intimate associate, and himself one of the most famous of American lawyers, says that "sometimes, after Lincoln entered upon a criminal case, the conviction that his client was guilty would affect him with a sort of panic. On one occasion he turned suddenly to his associate and said, 'Swett, the man is guilty; you defend him, I can't,' and so gave up his share of a large fee."

LINCOLN'S OWN STORIES

It was a common thing for Lincoln to discourage unnecessary lawsuits, and consequently he was continually sacrificing opportunities to make money. One man who asked him to bring suit for two dollars and a half against a debtor who had not a cent with which to pay, would not be put off in his passion for revenge. His counsel therefore gravely demanded ten dollars as a retainer. Half of this he gave to the poor defendant, who thereupon confessed judgment and paid the $2.50. Thus the suit was ended, to the entire satisfaction of the angry creditor.

The son of Jack Armstrong, the champion of Clary's Grove, whose loyal friendship Lincoln had won by whipping him in open battle at New Salem, was on trial for killing a man. Jack was in his grave, but his widow turned to Lincoln to save her boy. He gratefully remembered that the poor woman had been almost a mother to him in his friendless days and that her cabin had been his home when he had no other. He laid aside everything else and went to her aid. The defendant's guilt was extremely doubtful.

The chief witness testified that he saw the boy strike the fatal blow and that the affair occurred about eleven o'clock at night. Lincoln inquired how he could have seen so clearly at

THE LAWYER

that late hour. By the moonlight, the witness answered. Was there light enough to see everything that happened? Lincoln asked. The moon was about where the sun would be at ten o'clock in the morning and nearly full, the man on the stand replied. Almost instantly Lincoln held out a calendar. By this he showed that on the night in question the moon was only slightly past its first quarter, that it set within an hour after the fatal occurrence, and that it could therefore have shed little or no light on the scene of the alleged murder. The crowded court was electrified by the disclosure.

"Hannah," whispered Lincoln, as he turned to the mother, "Bill will be cleared before sundown." And he was.

An anecdote is related in connection with a case involving a bodily attack. Mr. Lincoln defended, and told the jury that his client was in the plight of a man who, in going along the highway with a pitchfork over his shoulder, was attacked by a fierce dog that ran out at him from a farmer's door-yard. In warding off the brute with the fork its prongs pierced and killed him.

"What made you kill my dog?" said the farmer.

"What made him bite me?"

"But why did you not go after him with the other end of the pitchfork?"

"Why did he not come at me with his other end?"

At this Mr. Lincoln whirled about, in his long arms an imaginary dog, and pushed his tail toward the jury. This was the defensive plea of "*Son assaut demesne*"—loosely, that "The other fellow brought on the fight" quickly told in a way the dullest mind would grasp and retain.

Gen. John H. Littlefield, who studied law with Abraham Lincoln, tells this anecdote in his recollections of this great figure: "All clients knew that, with 'Old Abe' as their lawyer, they would win their case—if it was fair; if not, that it was a waste of time to take it to him. After listening some time one day to a would-be client's statement, with his eyes on the ceiling, he swung around in his chair and exclaimed: 'Well, you have a pretty good case in technical law, but a pretty bad one in equity and justice. You'll have to get some other fellow to win this case for you. I couldn't do it. All the time while standing talking to that jury I'd be thinking, "Lincoln, you're a liar," and I believe I should forget myself and say it out loud.'"

THE LAWYER

This document, signed by Lincoln's old friend, Judge Davis, recalls a very interesting period of his early career while he was practising law on the old Eighth Circuit in Central Illinois. Lincoln and the Judge were fast friends from the beginning, the Judge having always evinced a particular appreciation of Lincoln's stories.

"I was never fined but once for contempt of court," says one of the clerks of the court in Lincoln's day. "Davis fined me five dollars. Mr. Lincoln had just come in, and leaning over my desk had told me a story so irresistibly funny that I broke out into a loud laugh. The Judge called me to order, saying, 'This must be stopped. Mr. Lincoln, you are constantly disturbing this court with your stories.' Then to me: 'You may fine yourself five dollars.' I apologized, but told the Judge the story was worth the money. In a few minutes the Judge called me to him. 'What was that story Lincoln told you?' he asked. I told him, and he laughed aloud in spite of himself. 'Remit your fine,' he ordered."

In the early days of Illinois, when Lincoln was a young lawyer, it was the custom of the profession to go from one county-seat to another for the trial of cases. These journeys were made on horseback, and on one occasion a party of lawyers, among them Mr. Lincoln, were riding across the country in the central part of the State.

The road took them through a grove, and as they passed along, a little bird which had fallen from the nest lay fluttering on the ground and was noticed by several of the horsemen, including Mr. Lincoln.

After riding a short distance he said to his companions, "Wait a moment, I want to go back," and as they stopped for him he was seen to ride back, dismount, and pick up the little fledgling and carefully put it in the nest.

When he rejoined the party they said: "Why, Lincoln, you need not have stopped for such a trifle as that," but, pausing a little while, he answered, quietly, "Well, I feel better for doing it, anyhow."

At the time of the first Republican Convention in Philadelphia, in 1856, Lincoln was following Judge Davis around the circuit in Illinois and attending a special term of the court in Urbana.

Mr. Whitney relates that Judge Davis and the non-resident lawyers were quartered at the leading hostelry of the place. Their slumbers in the early dawn having too often been disturbed by the tones of a vibrant gong summoning them to breakfast, they decided one morning that the

THE LAWYER

offending instrument must be removed or in some way forever silenced. By a majority vote Mr. Lincoln was chosen to carry out the decree. Accordingly, a little earlier than usual before noon that day, he was seen to leave the court-room and hasten to the hotel. Slipping unobserved into the dining-room, he managed to secure the gong, secreted it under his coat, and was in the act of making off with it when Whitney and Judge Davis suddenly appeared on the scene. The former held in his hand a copy of the Chicago *Tribune*, which had just reached town. It contained the surprising and gratifying announcement that Mr. Lincoln had received one hundred and ten votes for Vice-President at the Philadelphia Convention the day before.

"Great business, this," chuckled Davis, "for a man who aspires to be Vice-President of the United States!"

Lincoln only smiled. "Davis and I," declared Whitney, "were greatly excited, but Lincoln was listless and indifferent. His only response was:

"'Surely it ain't me; there's another great man named Lincoln down in Massachusetts. I reckon it's him.'"

Lincoln was once arguing a case against an opponent who tried to convince the jury that precedent is superior to law, and that custom makes things legal in all cases. Lincoln's reply was one of his many effective analogies in the form of a story.

Lincoln told the jury that he would argue the case in the same way as his opponent, and began:

"Old Squire Bagley, from Menard, came into my office one day and said:

"'Lincoln, I want your advice as a lawyer. Has a man what's been elected justice of the peace a right to issue a marriage license?'

"I told him no; whereupon the old squire threw himself back in his chair very indignantly and said:

"'Lincoln, I thought you was a lawyer. Now, Bob Thomas and me had a bet on this thing, and we agreed to let you decide; but if this is your opinion I don't want it, for I know a thunderin' sight better. I've been a squire eight years, and I've issued marriage licenses all the time.'"

One day Lincoln and a certain judge who was an intimate friend of his were bantering each other about horses, a favorite topic. Finally Lincoln said:

"Well, look here, Judge! I'll tell you what I'll do. I'll make a horse-trade with you, only it must be upon these stipulations: Neither party shall see the other's horse until it is produced here in the courtyard of the hotel and both parties must trade horses. If either party backs out of the agreement, he does so under a forfeiture of twenty-five dollars."

"Agreed," cried the judge, and both he and Lincoln went in quest of their respective animals.

A crowd gathered, anticipating some fun, and when the judge returned first the laugh was uproarious. He led, or rather dragged, at the end of a halter the meanest, boniest, rib-staring quadruped—blind in both eyes—that ever pressed turf. But presently Lincoln came along carrying over his shoulder a carpenter's sawhorse. Then the mirth of the crowd was furious. Lincoln solemnly set his horse down, and silently surveyed the judge's animal with a comical look of infinite disgust.

"Well, Judge," he finally said, "this is the first time I ever got the worst of it in a horse-trade."

Lincoln, who was one of the most generous and kind-hearted of men, often said that there was no act which was not prompted by some selfish motive. He was riding in a stage from Springfield, Illinois, to a neighboring town and was discussing this philosophy with a fellow-passenger.

As the stage rumbled past a ditch which was filled with mud and mire the passengers could see a small pig, caught fast in the muck, squealing and struggling to free himself. Many persons in the stage laughed heartily, but Mr. Lincoln, then a lawyer, asked the driver to stop for a few moments.

Leaping from the stage, he walked to the ditch over his shoetops in mud and picked the little animal up, setting it on the solid road.

"Now, look here," said the passenger with whom he had been talking, "you cannot say that was a selfish act."

"Extremely selfish," said Mr. Lincoln. "If I had left that little fellow in there the memory of his squealing would have made me uncomfortable all day. That is why I freed him."

He was a poor money-maker. Daniel Webster, who sent him a case, was amazed at the smallness of his bill, and his fellow-lawyers looked upon his charges as very low. This was his only fault, in their eyes. Once, when another attorney had collected $250 for their joint services, he refused to accept his share until the fee had been reduced to what he considered fair proportions and the

THE LAWYER

overcharge had been returned to the client. When David Davis, the presiding judge of the circuit, heard of this, he indignantly exclaimed, "Lincoln, your picayune charges will impoverish the bar."

He was equally ready to take up a just case without hope of pay as he was to refuse an unjust one even at the loss of a good fee. He once dragged into court a pension agent who insisted on keeping for himself half of a $400 claim which he had collected for a poor widow. There, in his own expressive phrase, he "skinned" him, moved the jury to tears by his stirring appeal for justice to the old woman, and won the verdict, all without charge to his client.

In another interesting and important case he laid down the rule that people had as much right to cross rivers as they had to go up and down them. This trial arose from the building of the first bridge over the Mississippi and from the fight which the boatmen made against it as an obstruction to their business.

Lincoln was once opposed to his former preceptor, Judge Logan, in the trial of a suit. Logan was a very dignified gentleman, but somewhat careless in matters of dress, often appearing with neither collar nor necktie. Lincoln, knowing his man, proceeded to undo him before the jury in the following manner:

"Gentlemen," began Lincoln, "you must be careful and not permit yourselves to be overborne by the eloquence of the counsel for defense. Judge Logan, I know, is an effective lawyer; I have met him too often to doubt that. But shrewd and careful though he be, still he is sometimes wrong. Since this trial began I have discovered that, with all his caution and fastidiousness, he hasn't knowledge enough to put his shirt on right."

It then transpired that Logan was wearing his shirt with the plaited bosom behind, and his embarrassment was so great and the laughter of the jury so uproarious, that he completely lost his balance and effectiveness during the remainder of the trial.

The terms of his partnership with Judge Logan are not known, but it is fair to assume that his share was a very small one, for the Judge was a very thrifty man and not given to generosity. And even after his marriage to Mary Todd, in 1842, Lincoln declined an invitation to Kentucky, saying "that he was so poor and made so

THE LAWYER

little headway that he dropped back in a month of idleness as much as he gained in a year's sowing."

No man had a greater respect for real learning, but for the display article he had naught but contempt. Once a lawyer arrayed against him made use of a Latin maxim for the evident purpose of impressing his hearers or to perplex Mr. Lincoln, to whom he said, "Is not that so?"

"If that is Latin," dryly said Lincoln, "I think you had better call another witness."

A young lawyer once asked Mr. Lincoln if the county-seat of Logan County was named after him. "Well, it was named after I was," he gravely replied.

Once opposing counsel objected to a juror on the ground that he knew Mr. Lincoln, and as this was a reflection upon the honor of a lawyer, Judge Davis promptly overruled the objection. But when Mr. Lincoln, following the example of his adversary, examined two or three of the jury and found that they knew his opponent, the Judge interfered.

"Now, Mr. Lincoln," he observed, severely,

"you are wasting time. The mere fact that a juror knows your opponent does not disqualify him."

"No, your Honor," responded Mr. Lincoln, dryly, "but I am afraid some of the gentlemen may *not* know him, which would place me at a disadvantage."

His advice to lawyers was sound and clear. Herndon quotes him as saying: "Don't shoot too high. Aim lower, and the common people will understand you. They are the ones you want to reach—at least they are the ones you ought to reach. The educated and refined people will understand you, anyway. If you aim too high, your ideas will go over the heads of the masses and only hit those who need no hitting."

Speaking of some lawyer whose name is unknown he said, "He can compress the most words into the smallest ideas of any man I ever met."

Herndon relates, as an instance of Lincoln's moral honesty and his horror of a lie, that he (Herndon) once drew up a dilatory plea for the purpose of delaying a case for another term. But when it came to Lincoln's attention he promptly repudiated it.

THE LAWYER

"Is this founded on fact?" Lincoln inquired, and when Herndon admitted it was done merely to save their client's interests, which might otherwise be endangered, Lincoln instantly replied:

"You know it is a sham, and a sham is very often but another name for a lie. Don't let it go on record. The cursed thing may come staring us in the face long after this suit is forgotten." And the plea was withdrawn.

This is a sample of the way business was conducted in the Illinois courts. "The first term of Davis's court that I attended," relates Major Whitney, "the Judge was calling through the docket for the first time, in order to dispose of such cases as could be handled summarily, and likewise to sort the chaff from the wheat, when he came across a long bill in chancery, drawn by an excellent but somewhat indolent lawyer. On glancing at it he exclaimed: 'Why, Brother Snap, how did you rake up energy enough to get up such a long bill?'

"'Dunno, Jedge,' replied the party addressed, squirming in his seat and uneasily scratching his head. The Judge unfolded and held up the bill. 'Astonishing, ain't it? Brother Snap did it. Wonderful—eh, Lincoln?'

"This amounted to an order on Lincoln for a joke at this point, and he was ready, of course—he had to be; he never failed. 'It's like the lazy preacher,' drawled he, 'that used to write long sermons, and the explanation was, he got to writin' and was too lazy to stop.'"

Here is a scene from the circuit graphically described by Whitney: "In the evening all assembled in the Judge's room, where the blazing fagots were piled high and the yule-log was in place, and there were no strays there, although the door was not locked. Davis's methods were known, and his companions well-defined, and if a novice came he soon found out both. For instance, an unsophisticated person might become attracted to the Judge's room by our noise, supposing it to be 'free for all.' If Davis wanted him he was warmly welcomed, the fatted calf was killed, and the ring put on his finger; but if he was really not desired he was frozen out by the Judge thus: 'Ah, stop a minute, Lincoln! Have you some business, Mr. Dusenberry?' If Mr. Dusenberry should venture, 'Well, no! I came designin'—" Davis would interrupt him: 'Swett, take Mr. Dusenberry out into the hall and see what he wants, and come right back yourself, Swett. Shut the door. Now, go

THE LAWYER

ahead, Lincoln! You got as far as—ha! ha! ha! "She slid down the hill, and—" But wait for Swett. Swett! Swett!' called he. 'Hill' (to Lamon), 'call Swett in. Now, Lincoln, go ahead (and so forth). 'She slid down the hill, you know. Ho! ho! ho!' Any one who knew Davis would recognize this. This was a characteristic scene with Lincoln as the headpiece, though we often discussed philosophy, politics, and other human interests."

Lincoln's guileless exterior concealed a great fund of shrewdness and common sense about ordinary matters, as well as genius in the higher realms.

"I remember once," writes Whitney, "that while several of us lawyers were together, including Judge Davis, Lincoln suddenly asked a novel question regarding court practice, addressed to no one particularly, to which the Judge, who was in the habit certainly of appropriating his full share of any conversation, replied, stating what he understood the practice should be. Lincoln thereat laughed and said: "I asked that question, hoping that you would answer. I have that very question to present to the court in the morning, and I am very glad to find out that the court is on my side."

LINCOLN'S OWN STORIES

A long letter about a law case, containing a desire to retain him, he returned with the indorsement: "Count me in.   A. LINCOLN."

His first pair of spectacles, which he purchased in a small shop in Bloomington, with the remark that he "had got to be forty-seven years old and kinder needed them," cost him thirty-seven and a half cents.

At one o'clock, on a night after Lincoln had been away for a week, his Springfield neighbor heard the sound of an ax. Looking out of his window, he saw Lincoln in the moonlight chopping wood for his solitary supper.

"We had concluded a murder case," writes Whitney, "once in Champaign at noon, in which we had no chance of acquittal, and hoped the jury would disagree. In the afternoon a young lawyer from another county was making a rousing speech in a whisky-selling case, although there was nothing to talk about; but the chap was 'wound up' for a big speech and he couldn't stop till he had run down. We were in one corner of the court-room, anxiously hoping that our jury, which still remained out, would stay so, and finally disagree. Meanwhile, we were

THE LAWYER

bored and amused at the Demosthenean effort going on in a plain case of selling whisky. 'I wish that fellow would stop,' said Lincoln. 'I am afraid our jury will agree for the sake of getting in to hear his speech.'

"At the White House once I was regaling him with local news from Champaign (which he was always ready to hear), and I said, 'Blank is dead; his extremely disloyal sentiments so provoked his neighbors that there was serious talk of inflicting vengeance on him, and he was found dead in bed—caused largely by fright.' This man was an old Whig friend of Lincoln, but the reason of his exit from life's trials amused him. His comment was, 'He died, then, to save his life, it seems.'"

Whitney says that one of the most obvious of Mr. Lincoln's peculiarities was his dissimilitude of qualities, or inequality of conduct, his dignity of deportment and action, interspersed with freaks of frivolity and inanity; his high inspiration and achievement, and his descent into the most primitive vales of listlessness and the most ridiculous buffoonery.

Lincoln once told this story: A balloon ascension occurred in New Orleans "befo' da wa'," and

LINCOLN'S OWN STORIES

after sailing in the air for several hours the aeronaut, who was arrayed in silks and spangles like a circus-performer, descended in a cotton-field, where a gang of slaves were at work. The frightened negroes took to the woods—all but one venerable darky, who was rheumatic and could not run, and who, as the resplendent aeronaut approached, having apparently just dropped from heaven, said, "Good mornin', Massa Jesus; how's yo' pa?"

A New York firm applied to Lincoln some years before he became President for information as to the financial standing of one of his neighbors. This was the answer:

"Yours of the 10th received. First of all, he has a wife and baby; together they ought to be worth $500,000 to any man. Secondly, he has an office in which there is a table worth $1.50 and three chairs worth, say, $1. Last of all, there is in one corner a large rat-hole, which will bear looking into.

"Respectfully,
"A. LINCOLN."

While walking along a dusty road in Illinois in his circuit days Lincoln was overtaken by a stranger driving to town. "Will you have the

THE LAWYER

goodness to take my overcoat to town for me?" asked Lincoln. "With pleasure; but how will you get it again?" "Oh, very readily. I intend to remain in it," was Lincoln's prompt reply.

"Billy," he said to his partner Herndon, "over sixteen years together, and we have not had a cross word during all that time, have we?"

"Not one."

"Don't take the sign down, Billy; let it swing, that our clients may understand that the election of a President makes no change in the firm of Lincoln & Herndon. If I live, I'm coming back, and we will go right on practising law as if nothing had ever happened." Then the two went down the stairs and across the town to the railroad station, Lincoln never to return alive.

Part III

LOCAL POLITICS AND THE DOUGLAS DEBATES

III

LOCAL POLITICS AND THE DOUGLAS DEBATES

IT is said that Lincoln's first speech was as follows. His friends thought he would be a good candidate for the Legislature, and they put him into nomination. He came from his retreat in the woodlands to a country town where he was to meet his opponent. As he approached the town he passed the house in which his antagonist dwelt. He saw rising from the roof a thin spire of iron, and said, "What's that?" "Oh," said his friend, "that is a lightning-rod," and he explained the use of the lightning-rod. Mr. Lincoln had never before seen such an appendage to a dwelling, and he thought over it a good deal until his time came to speak. The man against whom he was running was the first to occupy the platform, and he addressed his fellow-citizens by saying that he hoped they would not throw him overboard for this unknown man, whose life they didn't know and with whom they were not acquainted, who had come up here from the unexplored tracts of the wilderness. Mr. Lincoln arose and said, "Friends, you don't know very much about me. I haven't had all the advantages that some of you have had; but, if you did know everything about me that you might know, you would be sure that there was nothing in my character that made it necessary to put on my house a lightning-rod to save me from the just vengeance of Almighty God."

On another occasion, when Mr. Lincoln was going to a political convention, one of his rivals, a liveryman, provided him with a slow horse, hoping that he would not reach his destination in time. Mr. Lincoln got there, however, and when he returned with the horse he said, "You keep this horse for funerals, don't you?" "Oh no," replied the liveryman. "Well, I'm glad of that, for if you did you'd never get a corpse to the grave in time for the Resurrection."

When he went to the Legislature in 1854, after an absence of twelve years from that body, he got the indorsement of the Whigs and the Know-Nothings, and the latter sent a committee to him to acquaint him of their action. He rejected their support in the following whimsical fashion:

THE DOUGLAS DEBATES

"Who are the native Americans?" he asked, rather pointedly. "Do they not wear the breech clout and carry the tomahawk? We pushed them from their homes, and now turn upon others not fortunate enough to come over so early as we or our forefathers. Gentlemen of the committee, your party is wrong in principle." Then he told this story:

"I had some time ago an Irishman named Patrick cultivating my garden. One morning I went out to see how he was getting along. 'Mr. Lincoln, what do yez think of these Know-Nothings?' he inquired. I explained what they were trying to do, and asked Pat why he had not been born in America. 'Faith,' he replied, 'I wanted to, but me mother wouldn't let me.'"

To Speed he wrote, in 1855, trying to define his political faith, as follows:

"You inquire where I now stand. This is a disputed point. I think I am a Whig; but others say there are no Whigs, and that I am an Abolitionist. When I was at Washington I voted for the Wilmot Proviso as good as forty times; and I never heard of any one attempting to unwhig me for that. I now do no more than oppose the extension of slavery. I am not a Know-Nothing, that is certain. How could I be? How can any one who abhors the oppression of negroes be in favor of degrading classes of white people? Our progress in degeneracy appears to me to be pretty rapid. As a nation we began by declaring that 'All men are created equal.' We now practically read it, 'All men are created equal negroes.' When the Know-Nothings get control it will read, 'All men are created equal except negroes and foreigners and Catholics.' When it comes to this I shall prefer emigrating to some country where they make no pretense of loving liberty."

A good instance of the execution which Mr. Lincoln sometimes effected with a story occurred in the Legislature. There was a troublesome member from Wabash County who gloried particularly in being a "strict constructionist." He found something "unconstitutional" in every measure that was brought forward for discussion. He was a member of the Judiciary Committee, and was very apt, after giving every measure a heavy pounding, to advocate its reference to this committee. No amount of sober argument could floor the member from Wabash. At last he came to be considered a man to be silenced, and Mr. Lincoln was resorted to for an expedient by which this object might be accomplished. He soon afterward honored the draft made upon him.

A measure was brought forward in which Mr. Lincoln's constituents were interested, when the member from Wabash arose and discharged all his batteries upon its unconstitutional points. Mr. Lincoln then took the floor, and with the quizzical expression of features which he could assume at will, and a mirthful twinkle in his gray eyes, said: "Mr. Speaker, the attack of the member from Wabash on the constitutionality of this measure reminds me of an old friend of mine. He's a peculiar-looking old fellow, with shaggy, overhanging eyebrows and a pair of spectacles under them. [Everybody turned to the member from Wabash, and recognized a personal description.] One morning, just after the old man got up, he imagined, on looking out of his door, that he saw rather a lively squirrel on a tree near his house. So he took down his rifle and fired at the squirrel, but the squirrel paid no attention to the shot. He loaded and fired again and again, until, at the thirteenth shot, he set down his gun impatiently, and said to his boy, who was looking on:

" 'Boy, there's something wrong with this rifle.'

" 'Rifle's all right, I know 'tis,' responded the boy, 'but where's your squirrel?'

LINCOLN'S OWN STORIES

"'Don't you see him, humped up about halfway up the tree?' inquired the old man, peering over his spectacles and getting mystified.

"'No, I don't,' responded the boy; and then, turning and looking into his father's face, he exclaimed: 'I see your squirrel! You have been firing at a gnat on your eyebrow!'"

Ex-Senator Cullom tells this story: "When Mr. Lincoln was nominated for Congress, Tazewell County, in which we resided, was a county in Lincoln's district. When Mr. Lincoln came to Tazewell County, father took him in his carriage to his several appointments and generally presided at his meetings. I attended one of the meetings. When Mr. Lincoln was introduced, he spoke as follows:

"'Fellow-citizens, ever since I have been in Tazewell County my old friend, Major Cullom, has been taking me around. He has heard all my speeches, and the only way I can fool the old Major, and make him believe I am not making the same speech all the time, is to turn it "ind for ind" once in a while.'

"This was the beginning of the first political speech I ever heard Mr. Lincoln deliver. I distinctly remember his pronunciation, 'ind for ind.' You can imagine how that caught the crowd."

THE DOUGLAS DEBATES

The wonderful simplicity of his similes made Emerson compare him with Æsop. In one of his speeches in the Douglas debates, speaking of the suppression of political debate, he says: "These popular sovereigns are at their work, blowing out the moral lights around us."

And when he was in Congress he spoke of Polk's message with regard to the Mexican War as "the half-insane mumbling of a fever-dream." He also describes military glory as "the attractive rainbow that rises in showers of blood; the serpent's eye that charms to destroy." Speaking of the helplessness of the American slave, he says: "They have him in his prison-house. They have searched his person and have left no prying instrument with him. One after another they have closed the heavy iron doors upon him, and now they have him, as it were, bolted in with a lock of a hundred keys, which can never be unlocked without the concurrence of every key; the keys in the hands of a hundred different men, and they scattered to a hundred different and distant places; and they stand musing as to what invention, in all the dominions of mind and matter, can be produced to make the impossibility of his escape more complete than it is."

LINCOLN'S OWN STORIES

Here is his modest autobiography as contained in the *Congressional Directory:*

"Born February 12, 1809, in Hardin County, Kentucky.

Education, defective.

Profession, lawyer.

Have been a captain of volunteers in Black Hawk War.

Postmaster in a very small office.

Four times a member of the Illinois Legislature and a member of the Lower House of Congress."

He opposed the Mexican War while he was in Congress, though he consistently voted for all the supplies needful for the army. To the argument that the war was not one of aggression he replied that it reminded him of the Illinois farmer who insisted: "I ain't greedy 'bout land. I only want what jines mine."

And later on, though he accepted the results of the war with patriotic satisfaction, he was much pleased at the failure of the Administration to take advantage of its political opportunity and by the Whig nomination of General Taylor, and declared that that nomination "took the Democrats on their blind side."

The Congressional Library and the Library of the Supreme Court, with their great stores of

THE DOUGLAS DEBATES

books, were like a gold mine in his eyes. And in his Congressional term the attendants more than once were amused to see him tie up a lot of books in his bandanna handkerchief, stick his cane through the knot, and go forth to his boarding-house with the bundle over his shoulder, just as in other days he had carried his wardrobe while tramping from job to job.

Lincoln was much amused at this story, which he used to tell: In 1858 he had an appointment in Cumberland County, and after he had spoken a Dr. Hamburgher (a bitter Democrat) impudently jumped up and said he would reply. So Lincoln took a seat on the outer edge of the plank seat and listened.

Hamburgher presently got violent and insulting, when a little, insignificant-looking lame man jumped up to Lincoln and said: "Don't mind him; I know him; I live here; I'll take care of him; watch me." And two or three times he came to Lincoln and repeated the admonition. When Hamburgher concluded, the little lame man was on the platform and at once commenced a reply, and had proceeded but a short time when Hamburgher roared out: "That's a lie." "Never mind," retorted the lame man, patronizingly, "I'll take that from you—in fact,

I'll take anything from you except your pills." This cut the doctor to the raw. "You scoundrel!" exclaimed he, "you know I've quit practising medicine." The little lame man instantly dropped down on his sound knee and, raising his hands in mock worship, exclaimed: "Then, thank God, the country is safe!"

In the famous Douglas debates Judge Douglas called the Republican party the "allied army," and declared that he would deal with it "just as the Russians dealt with the allies at Sebastopol; that is, the Russians did not stop to inquire, when they fired a broadside, whether it hit an Englishman, a Frenchman, or a Turk." It was something more than a witticism when Lincoln rejoined, "In that case, I beg he will indulge us while we suggest to him that those allies took Sebastopol."

"Judge Douglas," said Mr. Lincoln in the same debate, "is of world-wide renown. All the anxious politicians of his party . . . have been looking upon as certainly . . . to be President of the United States. They have seen in his round, jolly, fruitful face post-offices, land offices, marshalships, and cabinet appointments, chargeships, and foreign missions bursting and spread-

THE DOUGLAS DEBATES

ing out in wonderful exuberance, ready to be laid hold of by their greedy hands. And as they have been gazing upon this attractive picture so long they cannot, in the little distraction that has taken place in the party, bring themselves to give up the charming hope, but with greedier anxiety they rush about him, sustain him and give him marches, triumphal entries and receptions, beyond what in the days of his highest prosperity they could have brought about in his favor. On the contrary, nobody has ever expected me to be President. In my poor, lean, lank face nobody has ever seen that any cabbages were sprouting."

In one of his debates with Stephen A. Douglas during that Senatorial campaign, Judge Douglas tried to dismiss from the people's mind Lincoln's apprehensions for the Union by urging the people to trust in Providence. To this Lincoln replied by saying that if the country acted upon this advice it might find itself in the fix of the old woman whose horse ran away with her in the buggy. She said that "she trusted in Providence till the britchin' broke and then she didn't know what on airth to do!"

His clear vision and cogent and earnest argumentation often led him to coin impressive axioms. At Peoria, in the Douglas debate, he said: "When the white man governs himself, that is self-government; but when he governs himself and also governs another man, that is more than self-government—that is despotism." "No man is good enough to govern another man without that other's consent."

"Repeal the Missouri Compromise, repeal all compromise; repeal the Declaration of Independence, repeal all past history, still you can't repeal human nature." "Our Republican robe is soiled and trailed in the dust. Let us purify it. Let us turn and wash it white in the spirit if not in the blood of the Revolution."

In the Douglas debates only once did he descend to personalities, and then so whimsically that the sting was taken out of the recrimination. He was, however, hard-driven and his patience sorely tried.

"I don't want to quarrel with him," he said, referring to Douglas; "I don't want to call him a liar, but when I come to square up to him, I don't know what else to call him."

In one of the Douglas debates he said that the judge ascribed some things to him by "mere burlesques on the art and name of argument—

THE DOUGLAS DEBATES

by such fantastic arrangements of words as prove horse-chestnuts to be chestnut horses."

On another occasion Douglas, in one of his speeches, made a strong point against Lincoln by telling the crowd that when he first knew Mr. Lincoln he was a "grocery-keeper," and sold whisky, cigars, etc. "Mr. L.," he said, "was a very good bartender!" This brought the laugh on Lincoln, whose reply, however, soon came, and then the laugh was on the other side.

"What Mr. Douglas has said, gentlemen," replied Lincoln, "is true enough; I did keep a grocery, and I did sell cotton, candles and cigars, and sometimes whisky; but I remember in those days that Mr. Douglas was one of my best customers. Many a time have I stood on one side of the counter and sold whisky to Mr. Douglas on the other side, but the difference between us now is this: I have left my side of the counter, but Mr. Douglas still sticks to his as tenaciously as ever."

On one occasion, when Lincoln and Douglas were "stumping" the State of Illinois together as political opponents, Douglas, who had the first speech, remarked that in early life his father, who he said was an excellent cooper by trade, apprenticed him out to learn the cabinet business.

This was too good for Lincoln to let pass, so when his turn came to reply he said:

"I had understood before that Mr. Douglas had been bound out to learn the cabinet-making business, which is all well enough, but I was not aware until now that his father was a cooper. I have no doubt, however, that he was one, and I am certain, also, that he was a very good one, for [here Lincoln gently bowed toward Douglas] he has made one of the best whisky casks I have ever seen."

As Douglas was a short, heavy-set man, and occasionally imbibed, the pith of the joke was all at once apparent, and most heartily enjoyed by all.

He did not believe in making voters of negroes—probably not at that stage of public opinion, for he said, "There is a physical difference between the white and black races which I believe will forever forbid the two races living together on social and political equality. However," he continued, "in the right to put into his mouth the bread that his own hands have earned, the negro is the peer of Judge Douglas or any other man."

THE DOUGLAS DEBATES

Colonel Lamon describes Douglas as always traveling in a special train decorated with banners and flags and accompanied by a brass band and an army of retainers. Lincoln, on the other hand, went by the ordinary train and ofttimes by freight, though the railroad company issued special orders that no passengers be permitted to travel by freight, and Lincoln had to use his great powers of persuasion. Much depended on the politics of the conductor. "Mr. Lincoln and I," Lamon writes in his Life of Lincoln, "with other friends, were traveling in the caboose of a freight train, when we were switched off the main track to allow a special train to pass in which Mr. Lincoln's more aristocratic rival was being conveyed. The passing train was decorated with banners and flags and carried a band of music which was playing, 'Hail to the Chief!' As the train whistled past, Mr. Lincoln broke out into a fit of laughter, and said, 'Boys, the gentleman in that car evidently smelt no royalty in our carriage.'"

Major Whitney tells an interesting incident of the debate:

"Lincoln and I were at the Centralia Agricultural Fair the day after the debate at Jonesboro. Night came on and we were tired, having been on the fair grounds all day. We were to go North on the Illinois Central Railroad. The train was due at midnight, and the depot was full of people. I managed to get a chair for Lincoln in the office of the superintendent of the railroad, but small politicians would intrude so that he could scarcely get a moment's sleep. The train came and was instantly filled. I got a seat near the door for Lincoln and myself. He was worn out and he had to meet Douglas the next day at Charleston. An empty car, called the saloon car, was hitched to the rear of the train and locked up. I asked the conductor, who knew Lincoln and myself well—we were both attorneys of the road—if Lincoln could not ride in that car; that he was exhausted and needed rest; but the conductor refused. I afterward got him in by stratagem. At the same time, George B. McClellan in person (then vice-president of the road) was taking Douglas around in a special car and a special train; and that was the unjust treatment Lincoln got from the Illinois Central Railroad."

On one occasion some of Lincoln's friends were talking of the diminutive stature of Stephen A. Douglas, and an argument as to the proper length

THE DOUGLAS DEBATES

of a man's legs. During the discussion Lincoln came in, and it was agreed that the question should be referred to him for decision.

"Well," said he, reflectively, "I should think a man's legs ought to be long enough to reach from his body to the ground."

Lincoln once commented on Douglas's position with regard to the extension of slavery into the Territories as follows:

"The Judge holds that a thing may be lawfully driven away from a place where it has a lawful right to be."

Another epigram, this speaking of Douglas's joint debates:

"Explanations explanatory of things explained."

His wonderful grasp of the political situation and of the slavery question is excellently illustrated in the following, from one of his speeches in the Douglas debate:

"The sum of pro-slavery theology seems to be this: 'Slavery is not universally right, nor yet universally wrong; it is better for some people to be slaves; and, in such cases, it is the will of God that they be such.' Certainly there is no contending against the will of God; but still there is some difficulty in ascertaining and applying it to particular cases. For instance, we will suppose the Rev. Dr. Ross has a slave named Sambo, and the question is, 'Is it the will of God that Sambo shall remain a slave, or be set free?' The Almighty gives no audible answer to the question, and His revelation, the Bible, gives none—or at most none but such that admits a squabble as to His meaning; no one thinks of asking Sambo's opinion on it. So at last it comes to this, that Dr. Ross is to decide the question; and while he considers it he sits in the shade, with gloves on his hands, and subsists on the bread that Sambo is earning in the burning sun. If he decides that God wills Sambo to continue a slave, he thereby retains his own comfortable position; but if he decides that God willed Sambo to be free, he thereby has to walk out of the shade, throw off his gloves, and delve for his own bread. Will Dr. Ross be actuated by the perfect impartiality which has ever been considered most favorable to correct decisions?"

Mr. Lincoln, being asked by a friend how he felt when the returns came in that insured his defeat for the Senate, replied that he felt, he supposed, very much like the stripling who had stumped his toe—too *badly* to *laugh* and too *big* to *cry*.

Speaking of the success of Judge Douglas and his own failure, he gave utterance to this noble sentiment: "I affect no contempt for the high eminence he has reached. So reached that the oppressed of my species might have shared with me in the elevation, I would rather stand on that eminence than wear the richest crown that ever pressed a monarch's brow."

Part IV
AT THE WHITE HOUSE

IV

AT THE WHITE HOUSE

THE President once related an incident that had occurred at Decatur when the Illinois Republicans named him as their choice for the Presidency. An old Democrat from "Egypt," as southern Illinois was called, approached Mr. Lincoln and said, "So you're Abe Lincoln?"

"Yes, that is my name."

"They say you're a self-made man."

"Well, yes; what there is of me is self-made."

"Well, all I've got to say," observed the old man, after a careful survey of the Republican candidate, "is that it was a d—d bad job."

When the Republican Convention of 1860 was about to be held in Chicago, Seward stayed at home in Auburn. When Lincoln was asked whether he would go to the Chicago Convention, he replied, quaintly, "I am a little too much of a candidate to go, and not quite enough of a candidate to stay away; but upon the whole I believe I will not go."

LINCOLN'S OWN STORIES

During the sitting of the Chicago Convention Lincoln had been trying, in one way or another, to keep down the excitement which was pent up within him by amusing himself and telling stories. When the news actually reached him he was in the editorial office of the *Journal*. He got up at once and allowed a little crowd to shake hands with him mechanically, then said:

"I reckon there's a little woman down at our house that would like to hear the news," and he started with rapid strides for home.

When it became an assured fact that he was elected, the President-elect got ready for his eastward journey, and he and Mrs. Lincoln paid a brief visit to Chicago, where his wife bought a silk dress for the inaugural ceremonies. When they got home, and were unpacking their purchases, Mr. Lincoln said: "Well, wife, there is one thing very likely to come out of this scrape, anyhow. We are going to have some new clothes."

It cannot be charged that Mr. Lincoln was a husband to grace fashionable society. He hated clothing of all sorts, and it was his habit, on reaching his office or his home, to take off his boots, as he naïvely expressed it, "to allow his feet to

AT THE WHITE HOUSE

breathe," and very often he would receive the friends of his wife at the door in his shirt-sleeves. He was a thoroughly informal man. At the time of the Chicago visit just referred to, a prominent lady called by appointment to see Mrs. Lincoln. He received the caller and, apologizing for his wife's tardiness, explained that she would be down "as soon as she got all her trotting harness on."

Soon after Lincoln's election he held a reception in the principal hotel in Chicago. For several hours a continuous procession of his friends and admirers passed before him, many of them old and intimate acquaintances. It was amusing to observe Lincoln's unfeigned enjoyment, and to hear his hearty greeting in answer to familiar friends who exclaimed, "How are you, Abe?" he, responding in like manner with "Hello, Bill!" or "Jack!" or "Tom!" alternately pulling or pushing them along with his powerful hand and arm, saying, "There's no time to talk now, boys; we must not stop this big procession, so move on."

One day after his election, while a group of distinguished politicians from a distance were sitting in the Governor's room at Springfield,

LINCOLN'S OWN STORIES

Ill., chatting with Lincoln, the door opened and an old lady in a big sunbonnet and the garb of a farmer's wife came in.

"I wanted to give you something to take to Washington, Mr. Lincoln," she said, "and these are all I had. I spun the yarn and knit them socks myself." And with an air of pride she handed him a pair of blue woolen stockings.

Lincoln thanked her cordially for her thoughtfulness, inquired after the folks at home, and escorted her to the door as politely as if she had been the Queen of England. Then, when he returned to the room, he picked up the stockings, held them by the toes, one in each hand, and with a queer smile upon his face remarked to the statesmen around him:

"The old lady got my latitude and longitude about right, didn't she?"

When the election was over and his friends begged him to assure the South that he contemplated no adverse action, he resisted the temptation and said that it reminded him of one of his experiences on the circuit when he saw a lawyer making frantic signals to an associate who was making blundering admissions to the jury, utterly oblivious of the wreck he was making of the case.

AT THE WHITE HOUSE

"Now, that's the way with Buchanan and me. He is giving the case away, and I can't stop him."

One of the most affecting and tenderest examples of Lincoln's oratory is his farewell speech to his Springfield friends and neighbors on the eve of his departure for Washington, February 11, 1861:

"My friends, no one not in my position can realize the sadness I feel at this parting. To this people I owe all that I am. Here I have lived more than a quarter of a century. Here my children were born, and here one of them lies buried. I know not how soon I shall see you again. I go to assume a task more difficult than that which has devolved upon any other man since the days of Washington. He never would have succeeded except for the aid of Divine Providence, upon which he at all times relied. I feel that I cannot succeed without the same Divine blessing which sustained him; and on the same Almighty Being I place my reliance for support. And I hope you, my friends, will all pray that I may receive that Divine assistance without which I cannot succeed, but with which success is certain. Again I bid you an affectionate farewell."

LINCOLN'S OWN STORIES

Upon Mr. Lincoln's arrival in Washington he immediately handed a copy of his inaugural address to his future Secretary of State, and the latter revised it in a vigorous and arrogant manner. Mr. Seward was always ready to offer advice and give directions upon every subject. Lincoln listened with respectful attention, but continued to exercise his own judgment, and the spirit of independence he showed concerning several matters which Mr. Seward undertook to decide for him so alarmed the latter that two days before the inauguration he wrote a polite note asking leave to withdraw his acceptance of the office of Secretary of State. The note was received on Saturday. Any other man but Lincoln would have been disconcerted at least, and would have immediately sought advice and assistance; but he did not mention the matter to any one, nor did he make any reply until Monday morning. Then, while waiting at Willard's Hotel for President Buchanan to escort him to the Capitol, he dictated a brief note, saying: "I feel constrained to beg that you will countermand the withdrawal. The public interest, I think, demands that you should, and my personal feelings are deeply enlisted in the same direction."

He handed the note to Mr. Nicolay, saying, "I can't afford to let Seward take the first trick."

AT THE WHITE HOUSE

While Mr. Lincoln was a man of great evenness of temper and kindness of disposition, he was at the same time a masterful man. He permitted no man to meddle with his official responsibilities. This is illustrated in the following story: Soon after the outbreak of the war, it is said that Secretary Seward advised the President to confine his energies solely to military and internal affairs, and to leave him (Seward) as prime minister, to deal with our foreign affairs. Mr. Seward proposed to submit his views on the subject in writing. The President assented. The story goes, that one day Seward called on the President with a voluminous paper which he had prepared, folded and indorsed. The President took it. In front of him, on his table, was a row of trays. They were labeled "Secretary of State," "Secretary of War," and so on, and the last tray was marked "Unimportant." Glancing along down the list to the last, the President plumped into it Mr. Seward's suggestions in writing, saying that if the things suggested by Mr. Seward must be done, he (the President) must do them. In that modest way he gave Mr. Seward to understand that the President was not delegating the responsibilities of his administration to any one else. Two months afterward Secretary Seward had become better acquainted with Mr. Lincoln, and in a letter to his wife he said, "The President is the best of us all."

Men rushed to the White House in offended dignity to complain of the high-handed measures of the new Secretary, Stanton. To smooth the ruffled feelings of one of them, Lincoln told a story. "We may," he said, "have to treat Stanton as they are sometimes obliged to treat a Methodist minister I know out West. He gets wrought up to so high a pitch of excitement in his prayers and exhortations that they put bricks in his pockets to keep him down. But I guess," the President concluded, with a twinkle, "we'll let him jump a while first."

The following story is told of the Hon. Peter Harvey, the friend and biographer of Daniel Webster:

Mr. Harvey was a very large man with a small voice and that pomposity of manner that very many diffident men possess. Above everything he valued and prized himself upon his friendship with the "Great Expounder."

The first year of the war he went to Washington, and on his return was asked how he liked President Lincoln.

"Well," he said, "Mr. Lincoln is a very sin-

AT THE WHITE HOUSE

gular man. I went on to see him, and told him that I'd been an intimate personal friend of Daniel Webster; that I had talked with him so much on the affairs of the country that I felt perfectly competent to tell him what Mr. Webster would advise in the present crisis; and thereupon I talked to Mr. Lincoln for two solid hours, telling him just what he should do and what he should not do; and would you believe it, sir, when I got through, all Mr. Lincoln said was, as he clapped his hand on my leg, 'Mr. Harvey, what tremendous great calves you have got!'"

At the opening of the administration he was overwhelmed with persistent office-seekers, and so much of his time was occupied in listening to their demands and trying to gratify them that he felt he was not attending to military affairs and matters of public policy as closely as he should. He compared himself to a man who was so busy letting rooms at one end of his house that he had no time to put out a fire that was destroying the other end. And when he was attacked with the varioloid in 1861 he said to his usher:

"Tell all the office-seekers to come and see me, for now I have something that I can give them."

LINCOLN'S OWN STORIES

The political problems alone would have been as great a load as mortal man might have been expected to carry, but his perplexities were increased, his time occupied, and his patience sorely tested by such an undignified and unpatriotic clamor for offices as has never been exceeded in the history of our government. The Democratic party had been in power for many years. Every position in the gift of President Buchanan had been filled with a Democrat, many of them Southern sympathizers, and now hordes of hungry Republicans besieged the White House demanding appointments. The situation was described by the President in a single ejaculation. A Senator who noticed an expression of anxiety and dejection upon his face inquired:

"Has anything gone wrong, Mr. President? Have you heard bad news from Fort Sumter?"

"No," answered the President, solemnly, "it's the post-office at Jonesville, Missouri."

There was an ignorant man who once applied to Lincoln for the post of doorkeeper to the House. This man had no right to ask Lincoln for anything. It was necessary to repulse him. But Lincoln repulsed him gently and whimsically, without hurting his feelings, in this way:

AT THE WHITE HOUSE

"So you want to be doorkeeper of the House, eh?"

"Yes, Mr. President."

"Well, have you ever been a doorkeeper? Have you ever had any experience of doorkeeping?"

"Well, no—no actual experience, sir."

"Any theoretical experience? Any instructions in the duties and ethics of doorkeeping?

"Umph—no."

"Have you ever attended lectures on doorkeeping?"

"No, sir."

"Have you read any text on the subject?"

"No."

"Have you conversed with any one who has read such a book?"

"No, sir; I'm afraid not, sir."

"Well, then, my friend, don't you see that you haven't a single qualification for this important post?" said Lincoln, in a reproachful tone.

"Yes, I do," said the applicant, and he took leave humbly, almost gratefully.

A delegation once waited upon Mr. Lincoln to ask the appointment of a gentleman as Commissioner to the Sandwich Islands.

LINCOLN'S OWN STORIES

Besides his fitness for the place they urged his bad health. The President said:

"Gentlemen, I am sorry to say that there are eight other applicants for that place and they are all sicker than your man."

To a member of Congress who applied to him for a mess of patronage he said: "Your demand illustrates the difference between the abstract and the concrete. When a bill is pending to create more army officers you take the floor and denounce it (although you dodge a vote on it) as a needless scheme to increase the power and tyranny of the Executive; but as soon as the bill becomes a law you come here and demand that all your brothers-in-law and cousins and nephews be appointed under it: your action in Congress is abstract, but in the Executive Chamber is concrete."

Thurlow Weed relates that he was one day opposing the claims of Montgomery Blair, who aspired to a Cabinet appointment, when Mr. Lincoln inquired of him whom he would recommend. "Henry Winter Davis," was the response. "David Davis, I see, has been posting you up on this question," retorted Lincoln. "He has Davis on the brain. I think

AT THE WHITE HOUSE

Maryland must be a good State to move from."

The President then told a story of a witness in court in a neighboring county, who, on being asked his age replied, "Sixty." Being satisfied he was much older, the question was repeated, "The court knows you to be much older than sixty." "Oh, I understand now," was the rejoinder, "you're thinking of those ten years I spent on the eastern shore of Maryland; that was so much time lost, and don't count."

"The Democrats must vote to hold the Union now," he once said, referring to the political situation, "without bothering whether we or the Southern men got things where they are. And we must make it easy for them to do this, for we cannot live through the case without them."

He then told about the Illinois man who was chased by a fierce bull in a pasture, and, dodging around a tree, caught the tail of the pursuing beast. After pawing the earth for a time the bull broke away on a run, snorting at every jump, while the man clinging to its tail cried out, "Darn you, who commenced this fuss?" A remarkably clear view of the case.

LINCOLN'S OWN STORIES

Could any (even a professional) wag take off the swagger of a certain New Jersey Congressman better than this? He called on the President with two of his constituents, in order to see Lincoln as they would a show. "Mr. President," said he, "this is Mr. X and Mr. Y, and they are among the weightiest men in Southern New Jersey." After they had gone Lincoln said, "I wonder that end of the State didn't tip up when they got off it."

Once, as Lincoln was passing along Pennsylvania Avenue, a man came running after him, hailed him, and thrust a bundle of papers into his hand, requesting consideration for some petty office. It angered him not a little, and he pitched the papers back, saying, "I'm not going to open shop here."

A Western Senator who had failed of a reelection brought his successor, one day, and introduced him to the President. Lincoln, in reply, expressed his gratification at making the acquaintance of a new Senator. "Yet," he added, "I hate to have old friends like Senator W—— go away. And—another thing—I usually find that a Senator or Representative out of business is a sort of lame duck. He has to be provided

AT THE WHITE HOUSE

for." When the two gentlemen had withdrawn I took the liberty of saying that Mr. W—— did not seem to relish that remark. Weeks after, when I had forgotten the circumstance, the President said, "You thought I was almost rude to Senator W—— the other day. Well, now he wants Commissioner Dole's place!" Mr. Dole was then Commissioner of Indian Affairs.

It is said that Lincoln very seldom invented a story. Once he said: "You speak of Lincoln stories. I don't think that is a correct phrase. I don't make the stories mine by telling them. I'm only a retail dealer."

Scripture stories and incidents were also used by Lincoln to illustrate his argument or to enforce a point. Judge E—— had been concerned in a certain secret organization of "radical" Republicans, whose design was to defeat Lincoln's renomination. When this futile opposition had died out the Judge was pressed by his friends for a profitable office. Lincoln appointed him, and to one who remonstrated against such a display of magnanimity he replied: "Well, I suppose Judge E——, having been disappointed before, did behave pretty ugly; but that wouldn't make him any less fit for this place, and I have

Scriptural authority for appointing him. You remember that when Moses was on Mount Sinai, getting a commission for Aaron, that same Aaron was at the foot of the mountain making a false god for the people to worship. Yet Aaron got his commission, you know."

The late Chief-Justice Carter, of the District of Columbia, once called upon Lincoln with a party of politicians to secure the appointment of a gentleman who was opposed by the Senators from his State. Lincoln suggested that they ought to get the Senators on their side. They replied that, owing to local complications, such a thing was impossible. Lincoln retorted that nothing was impossible in politics; that the peculiarities of the Senator referred to were well known, and that by the use of a little tact and diplomacy he might be brought around, in which case there would be no doubt about the appointment. To clinch his argument, Lincoln told a story of James Quarles, a distinguished lawyer of Tennessee. Quarles, he said, was trying a case, and after producing his evidence rested; whereupon the defense produced a witness who swore Quarles completely out of court, and a verdict was rendered accordingly. After the trial one of his friends came to him and said:

AT THE WHITE HOUSE

"Why didn't you get that feller to swar on your side?"

"I didn't know anything about him," replied Quarles.

"I might have told you about him," said the friend, "for he would swar for you jest as hard as he'd swar for the other side. That's his business. Judge, that feller takes in swarin' for a livin'."

Anthony J. Bleecker tells his experience in applying for a position under Mr. Lincoln. The President requested him to read his vouchers. Before Bleecker got half through the President cried out, "Oh, stop! You are like the man who killed the dog." "In what respect?" said Bleecker, not feeling particularly flattered by the comparison. Mr. Lincoln replied: "He had a vicious animal which he determined to despatch, and accordingly knocked out its brains with a club. He continued striking the dog until a friend stayed his hand, exclaiming, 'You needn't strike him any more — the dog is dead; you killed him at the first blow.' 'Oh yes,' said he, 'I know that; but I believe in punishment after death.' So, I see, do you."

Mr. Bleecker acknowledged that it was possible to do too much sometimes, and he in his turn told an anecdote of a good priest who converted an Indian from heathenism to Christianity; the only difficulty he had with him was to get him to pray for his enemies. "The Indian had been taught by his father to overcome and destroy them. 'That,' said the priest, 'may be the Indian's creed, but it is not the doctrine of Christianity or the Bible. St. Paul distinctly says, "If thine enemy hunger, feed him; if he thirst, give him drink."' The Indian shook his head at this and seemed dejected; but when the priest added, 'For in so doing thou shalt heap coals of fire upon his head,' the poor convert was overcome with emotion, fell on his knees, and with outstretched hands and uplifted eyes invoked all sorts of blessings on his adversary's head, supplicating for pleasant hunting-grounds, a large supply of squaws, lots of papooses, and all other Indian comforts, till the good priest interrupted him (as you did me), exclaiming, 'Stop, my son! You have discharged your Christian duty, and have done more than enough.' 'Oh no, Father,' says the Indian, 'let me pray! I want to burn him down to the stump!'"

Mr. Bleecker got the job.

"On arriving at the White House," relates General Wilson, "I found a Congressman in

AT THE WHITE HOUSE

earnest conversation with the President. Looking at me as if I were an intruder, the politician stopped, and Mr. Lincoln said, 'It is all right—we are going out together; so turn on your oratory.' So the member resumed talking vigorously for five minutes or more, in behalf of his constituent, an applicant for some office. The President, looking critically at the right side of his face and then on the left, remarked, in an interested manner, 'Why, how close you do shave, John!' That was the way in which he baffled the office-seekers; and, although the Congressman was disappointed, of course, he could not avoid laughing. After his departure I said, 'Mr. President, is that the way you manage the politicians?' And he answered, 'Well, you must not suppose you have all the strategy in the army.'"

H. C. Whitney relates the following story: "I was in Washington in regard to the Indian service for a few days in 1861, and I said to Mr. Lincoln one day, 'Everything is drifting into the war, and I guess you'll have to put me in the army.' He looked up from his work and said, good-humoredly: 'I'm making generals now. In a few days I'll be making quartermasters, and then I'll fix you.'"

LINCOLN'S OWN STORIES

Certain officials in the government employ were very anxious to get absolute control of certain moneys to be disbursed by them. These moneys were formerly controlled by the district attorneys of certain districts, and the control of these district attorneys they were anxious to set aside, and they came to the President with this plea. He knew what they wanted, and told them the following story:

"You are very much like a man in Illinois whose cabin was burned down, and, according to the kindly custom of early days in the West, his neighbors all contributed something to start him again. In his case they had been so liberal that he soon found himself better off than before the fire, and got proud. One day a neighbor brought him a bag of oats, but the fellow refused it with scorn, and said, 'I am not taking oats now; I take nothing but money.'"

While Lincoln was always very patient, he often adopted droll methods of getting rid of bores. The late Justice Carter of the Supreme Court of the District of Columbia used to relate an incident of a Philadelphia man who called at the White House so frequently, and took up so much of the President's time, that the latter finally lost his patience. One day when the

AT THE WHITE HOUSE

gentleman was particularly verbose and persistent, and refused to leave, although he knew that important delegations were waiting, Lincoln arose, walked over to a wardrobe in the corner of the Cabinet chamber, and took a bottle from a shelf. Looking gravely at his visitor, whose head was very bald, he remarked:

"Did you ever try this stuff for your hair?"

"No, sir, I never did."

"Well," remarked Lincoln, "I advise you to try it, and I will give you this bottle. If at first you don't succeed, try, try again. Keep it up. They say it will make hair grow on a pumpkin. Now take it and come back in eight or ten months and tell me how it works."

The astonished Philadelphian left the room instantly without a word, carrying the bottle in his hand, and Judge Carter, coming in with the next delegation, found the President doubled up with laughter at the success of his strategy. Before he could proceed to business the story had to be told.

He had a soft spot in his heart for the wounded soldiers who were incapacitated for duty, or, for that matter, for any kind of usefulness, as this message to the Senate will prove:

"Yesterday little indorsements of mine went

to you in two cases of postmasterships sought for widows whose husbands have fallen in the battles of this war. These cases occurring on the same day brought me to reflect more attentively than I had before done as to what is fairly due from us here in the dispensing of patronage to the men who, by fighting our battles, bear the chief burden of saving our country. My conclusion is that, other claims and qualifications being equal, they have the better right; and this is especially applicable to the disabled soldier and the deceased soldier's family."

"Soon after the opening of Congress, the Hon. Mr. Shannon made the customary call," writes Carpenter, the artist, "at the White House. In the conversation that ensued Mr. Shannon said, 'Mr. President, I met an old friend of yours in California last summer, a Mr. Campbell, who had a good deal to say about your Springfield life.' 'Ah!' returned Mr. Lincoln, 'I am glad to hear of him. Campbell used to be a dry fellow in those days,' he continued. 'For a time he was Secretary of State. One day during the legislative vacation a meek, cadaverous-looking man, with a white neck-cloth, introduced himself to him at his office, and, stating that he had

AT THE WHITE HOUSE

been informed that Mr. C. had the letting of the Hall of Representatives, he wished to secure it, if possible, for a course of lectures he desired to deliver in Springfield. "May I ask," said the Secretary, "what is to be the subject of your lecture?" "Certainly," was the reply, with a very solemn expression of countenance. "The course I wish to deliver is on the second coming of our Lord." "It is of no use," said C.; "if you will take my advice, you will not waste your time in this city. It is my private opinion, if the Lord has been in Springfield once, he will never come the second time!"'"

"One evening the President brought a couple of friends into the 'state dining-room' to see my picture," relates Carpenter. "Something was said, in the conversation that ensued, that 'reminded' him of the following circumstance: 'Judge ——,' said he, 'held the strongest ideas of rigid government and close construction that I ever met. It was said of him, on one occasion, that he would hang a man for blowing his nose in the street, but he would quash the indictment if it failed to specify which hand he blew it with!'"

Lord Lyons, the British minister in Washington, once presented the President with an autograph letter from Queen Victoria announcing, as is the custom of European monarchs, the marriage of the Prince of Wales, and added that whatever response the President would make he would immediately transmit. Mr. Lincoln responded by shaking the marriage announcement at the bachelor minister before him, saying, "Lyons, go thou and do likewise."

For some men Lincoln had special uses, and his relations with them were limited to that narrow utility; for others his affinity was catholic. To an intimate who had mistakenly supposed that he placed much reliance on the counsels of David Davis, Judge of the Circuit Court, he explained away the error by this illustration. "They had side judges down in New Hampshire, and to show the folly of the system one who had been a side judge for twenty years said the only time the chief judge ever consulted him was at the close of a long day's session, when he turned to the side judge and whispered, 'Don't your back ache?'" And Davis himself relates that Lincoln never consulted him but once or twice.

Noah Brooks relates that when he had been at some pains, one day, to show the President

AT THE WHITE HOUSE

how a California politician had been coerced into telling the truth without knowing it, Lincoln said it reminded him of a black barber in Illinois, notorious for lying, who, hearing some of his customers admiring the planet Jupiter, then shining in the evening sky, said: "Sho, I've seen that star afore. I seen him 'way down in Georgy." The President continued: "Like your California friend, he told the truth, but thought he was lying."

A New-Yorker at the White House said to the President that it seemed strange that the President of the United States and the President of the Confederate States should have been born in the same State.

"Oh, I don't know about that," laughed Mr. Lincoln. "Those Kentucky people will tell you that they raise 'most anything in their State, and I reckon they're mighty near right."

There was very little social life in the White House during the Lincoln administration. The President gave a few state dinners each year, such as were required by his official position, held a few public receptions to gratify the curiosity of the Washington people and strangers in the city, and gave one ball, which excited much criticism from the religious press and from unfriendly sources. It was represented as a heartless exhibition of frivolity in the midst of dying soldiers and a grief-stricken country, and some people even went so far as to declare the death of Willie Lincoln, about two weeks later, to be a judgment of God upon the President and Mrs. Lincoln for indulging in worldly amusements. These thoughtless writers did not know that during the reception, which was in honor of the diplomatic corps, the President and Mrs. Lincoln both slipped away from their guests to spend a moment at the bedside of their child, who was so ill that the postponement of the entertainment was proposed, but vetoed by the President. The death of this lad was the greatest sorrow that ever fell upon the President's heart.

The great public receptions, with their vast, rushing multitudes pouring past him to shake hands, he rather enjoyed; they were not a disagreeable task to him, and he seemed surprised when people commiserated him upon them. He would shake hands with thousands of people, seemingly unconscious of what he was doing, murmuring some monotonous salutation as they went by, his eye dim, his thoughts far withdrawn; then suddenly he would see some familiar

AT THE WHITE HOUSE

face—his memory for faces was very good—and his eye would brighten and his whole form grow attentive; he would greet the visitor with a hearty grasp and a ringing word and dismiss him with a cheery laugh that filled the Blue Room with infectious good-nature. Many people armed themselves with an appropriate speech to be delivered on these occasions, but unless it was compressed into the smallest possible space it never was uttered; the crowd would jostle the peroration out of shape. If it were brief enough and hit the President's fancy, it generally received a swift answer. One night an elderly gentleman from Buffalo said, "Up our way we believe in God and Abraham Lincoln," to which the President replied, shoving him along the line, "My friend, you are more than half right."

He had a rule for evading difficulties which was expressed in a homely remark to Mr. Seward, who jokingly remarked at a Cabinet meeting one day:

"Mr. President, I hear that you turned out for a colored woman on a muddy crossing the other day."

"I don't remember," answered Lincoln, musingly, "but I think it very likely, for I have always made it a rule that if people won't turn out for me I will for them. If I didn't, there would be a collision."

Robert Dale Owen, the spiritualist, once read the President a long manuscript on an abstruse subject with which that rather erratic person loved to deal. Lincoln listened patiently until the author asked for his opinion, when he replied with a yawn:

"Well, for those who like that sort of thing I should think it is just about the sort of thing they would like."

Colonel Lamon in his *Recollections* tells this: A certain Washington police officer, who it seems was on intimate terms with the President, had accidentally killed a rough while making his arrest, and, though it was two o'clock in the morning, repaired at once to the White House, and requested Lincoln to come into his office. Mr. Lincoln heard his story, and observed that he had only done his duty. "It isn't that," answered the officer; "I know I did my duty, but I felt so badly over the affair that I wanted to talk to you about it." "Well," answered Lincoln, "go home now and get some sleep, but the next time you hit a man, don't hit him with

AT THE WHITE HOUSE

your fist. Hit him with a club or a crowbar, or something that won't kill him."

When he came to New York early in the sixties he went to hear Henry Ward Beecher, and afterward visited Five Points, then a most notorious slum. He was called upon to address the children, and his homely and kindly talk so pleased them that when he stopped they cried, "Go on," "Oh, do go on." As he was leaving the room the teacher asked him his name.

"Abraham Lincoln, from Illinois," he answered simply, and added nothing more.

After his great triumph in New York he spoke in many New England towns. Probably the greatest tribute to his powers as a speaker was paid by a professor at Yale College who observed with much admiration the fine structure of his speech. The professor took notes of the speech, and held it up before his class the next day as a model of English composition. He followed Lincoln to a neighboring city, that he might again sit at the feet of this master, self-taught in the mother-tongue.

Toward the end of 1862 the Cabinet crisis reached a climax, and a Senate committee urged

LINCOLN'S OWN STORIES

the President to reconstruct his Cabinet. However, he valued Seward and Chase too highly to part with them, and he met the situation in his own shrewd way. After it was all over, he said, referring to the interview: "While they seemed to believe in my honesty, they appeared to think that when I had in me any good purpose or intention Seward contrived to suck it out of me unperceived."

Without going into details, it is familiar history that the final result of the complaint was that both Seward and Chase resigned. Thus armed, Lincoln was in a position to satisfy both wings of the party. "Now I can ride, for I have a pumpkin in each bag," he shrewdly expressed it. Later he said wisely, in summing up the situation: "If I had yielded to that storm and dismissed Seward, the thing would all have slumped over one way, and we should have been left with a scanty handful of supporters. When Chase gave in his resignation, I saw that the game was in my hands, and I put it through."

To a deputation who urged that his Cabinet should be reconstructed after the retirement of Secretary Cameron the President told this story: "Gentlemen, when I was a young man I used to know very well one Joe Wilson, who built him-

AT THE WHITE HOUSE

self a log cabin not far from where I lived. Joe was very fond of eggs and chickens, and he took a very great deal of pains in fitting up a poultry-shed. Having at length got together a choice lot of young fowls—of which he was very proud—he began to be much annoyed by the depredations of certain little black and white spotted animals which it is not necessary to name. One night Joe was awakened by an unusual cackling and fluttering among his chickens. Getting up, he crept out to see what was going on. It was a bright moonlight night, and he soon caught sight of half a dozen of the little pests, which, with their dam, were running in and out of the shadow of the shed. Very wrathy, Joe put a double charge into his old musket and thought he would 'clean out' the whole tribe at one shot. Somehow he only killed one, and the balance scampered off across the field. In telling the story Joe would always pause here and hold his nose. 'Why didn't you follow them up and kill the rest?' inquired his neighbors. 'Blast it,' said Joe, 'it was eleven weeks before I got over killin' one. If you want any more skirmishing in that line you can do it yourselves!'"

Once a friend complained to the President that a certain Cabinet officer was administering his office with unusual energy, in the hope of securing the Presidential nomination.

"That reminds me," said Mr. Lincoln, "that my brother and I were once plowing a field with a lazy horse, but at times he rushed across the field so fast that I could hardly keep up with him. At last I found an enormous chin-fly on him, and knocked it off. Now I am not going to make that mistake a second time. If the Secretary has a chin-fly on him I am not going to knock it off, if it will only make his department go."

This is related by Gen. James Grant Wilson:

"Among several good things, the President told of a southern Illinois preacher who, in the course of his sermon, asserted that the Saviour was the only perfect man who had ever appeared in this world; also that there was no record, in the Bible or elsewhere, of any perfect woman having lived on the earth. Whereupon there arose in the rear of the church a persecuted-looking personage who, the parson having stopped speaking, said, 'I know a perfect woman, and I've heard of her every day for the last six years.' 'Who was she?' asked the minister. 'My husband's first wife,' replied the afflicted female."

"I once knew," said Lincoln, "a sound churchman by the name of Brown, who was a member

AT THE WHITE HOUSE

of a very sober and pious committee having in charge the erection of a bridge over a dangerous and rapid river. Several architects failed, and at last Brown said he had a friend named Jones who had built several bridges and undoubtedly could build that one. So Mr. Jones was called in.

"'Can you build this bridge?' inquired the committee.

"'Yes,' replied Jones, 'or any other. I could build a bridge to the infernal regions, if necessary.'

"The committee were shocked, and Brown felt called upon to defend his friend. 'I know Jones so well,' said he, 'and he is so honest a man and so good an architect that if he states soberly and positively that he can build a bridge to— to—why, I believe it; but I feel bound to say that I have my doubts about the abutment on the infernal side.'

"So," said Mr. Lincoln, "when politicians told me that the Northern and Southern wings of the Democracy could be harmonized, why, I believed them, of course; but I always had my doubts about the 'abutment' on the *other* side."

James Morgan tells, in his excellent *Life,* of Lincoln's freedom from the usual official vanity.

He rather shrank from than courted the official title of Mr. President, and generally referred to his office as "this place," "since I have been in this place," or, "since I came here." Referring at one time to the apartment reserved in the Capitol for the Chief Magistrate, he called it "the room, you know, that they call the President's room." Once he pleaded with some old Illinois friends who addressed him as Mr. President, "Now call me Lincoln, and I'll promise not to tell of the breach of etiquette."

Another story told by Morgan illustrates his inherent democracy. He dreamed he was in some great assembly, and the people drew back to let him pass, whereupon he heard some one say, "He is a common-looking fellow." In his dream Lincoln turned to the man and said, "Friend, the Lord prefers common-looking people; that is the reason why He made so many of them."

His receptions he called his "public-opinion baths." He said he came out of them with a renewed sense of his official obligations. "No hours of my day are better employed than those which bring me again within the direct contact and the atmosphere of the average of our whole people," he said, and added that they helped

AT THE WHITE HOUSE

"to renew in me a clearer and more vivid image of that great popular assemblage out of which I sprang and to which I must return." This is pure democracy, and certainly a patriotic interpretation of public duty.

Senator Charles Sumner of Massachusetts called at the White House early one morning. He was told that the President was down-stairs, that he could go right down. He found the President polishing his boots. Somewhat amazed, Senator Sumner said, "Why, Mr. President, do you black your own boots?" With a vigorous rub of the brush, the President replied, "Whose boots did you think I blacked?"

But he knew how to be correct in deportment when he deemed that occasion required it. A man who was present once when Charles Sumner called, has described the manner in which Lincoln received that self-conscious statesman. He dropped his long legs from the arm of the chair in which he was slouching at ease, rose and saluted with studied dignity his imposing caller, who carried a cane and was arrayed in a brown coat and fancy waistcoat, checked lavender trousers, and a striking pair of spats. After the Senator had gone Lincoln again relaxed, with the remark,

"When with the Romans we must do as the Romans do."

War maps hung on the walls of his office, and his table was covered so deep with papers that it was not always possible for him to find room to rest his hand while signing his name to a document. "I am like the Patagonians," he said with a laugh, once, as he hunted for a place where he could write. "You know they live off oysters, and throw the shells out of the window. When the pile of shells grows so high as to shut in the window, they simply move and build a new house."

Some gentlemen, fresh from a Western tour, calling at the White House to see President Lincoln, referred to a body of water in Nebraska bearing an Indian name which they could not recall, but which signified Weeping Water. Instantly Mr. Lincoln replied, "As Laughing Water, according to Mr. Longfellow, is Minnehaha, this must be Minneboohoo."

A friend discovered the President one day counting greenbacks. "The President of the United States has a multiplicity of duties not specified in the Constitution or the laws," said

AT THE WHITE HOUSE

Mr. Lincoln. "This is one of them. This money belongs to a negro porter in the Treasury Department who is now in the hospital so sick that he cannot sign his name. According to his wish, I am putting a part of it aside in an envelop, labeled, to save it for him."

Abraham Lincoln once received a letter asking for a "sentiment" and his autograph. He replied: "Dear Madam,—When you ask a stranger for that which is of interest only to yourself, always inclose a stamp. ABRAHAM LINCOLN."

He laughed at Senator Mason, who, on account of this sectional warfare, wore homespun to avoid buying goods of Northern manufacture. Mr. Lincoln said: "To carry out this idea he ought to go barefoot. If that's the plan, they should begin at the foundation and adopt the well-known 'Georgia costume' of a shirt-collar and a pair of spurs."

In 1864 five six-footers, accompanied by two representatives, called on the President and were introduced to him. These six-footers seemed to astonish Lincoln, who, after a careful survey, exclaimed, "Are they all from your State?"
"All."

LINCOLN'S OWN STORIES

"Why, it seems to me," said the President, glancing at the short Representatives, "that your State always sends her little men to Congress."

Lincoln once told the telegraph-operators in the War Department that the concise phraseology of the official despatches reminded him of the story of a Scotch girl who, on her way to market one morning, while fording a stream, was accosted by a countryman on the bank. "Good morning, my lassie," said he. "How deep's the brook, and what's the price of eggs?" "Knee-deep and a sixpence!" answered the little maid without looking up.

"The Wade and Davis matter troubles me little," said Lincoln to a friend. "Indeed, I feel a good deal about it as the old man did about his cheese when his very smart boy found, by the aid of a microscope, that it was full of maggots. 'Oh, father!' exclaimed the boy, 'how can you eat such stuff? Just look in here and see 'em wriggle.' The old man took another mouthful, and putting his teeth into it, replied grimly, 'Let 'em wriggle.'"

From a reply to an invitation to attend a festival in honor of the anniversary of Jefferson's birthday:

AT THE WHITE HOUSE

"I remember once being much amused at seeing two partially intoxicated men engaged in a fight with their coats on, which fight, after a long and harmless contest, resulted in each having fought himself out of his coat and into that of the other. If the two leading parties of this day are really identical with the two of the days of Jefferson and Adams, they have performed the same feat as the two drunken men."

Gen. O. O. Howard is responsible for this:
"In the first speech I ever saw of Mr. Lincoln's he said, 'Many free countries have lost their liberties, and ours may lose hers; but if she shall, be it my proudest boast not that I was the last to desert, but that I never, never deserted her.' That was valor."

A well-known literary man was praising Lincoln at a dinner in New York. "Lincoln," said he, "could not stand tedious writing in others. He once condemned for its tediousness a Greek history, whereupon a diplomat took him to task. 'The author of that history, Mr. President,' he said, 'is one of the profoundest scholars of the age. Indeed, it may be doubted whether any man of our generation has plunged more deeply in the sacred fount of learning.' 'Yes, or come up drier,' said Lincoln."

Lincoln had a genius for terseness. Never a wasted word and every word packed with meaning. Here is his definition of wealth. To him it was, as he once said, "simply a superfluity of things we don't need."

His moral honesty was like unto one of the prophets of old. When his friends urged him not to make his famous "house divided against itself" speech, he said: "Friends, the time has come when these sentiments should be uttered, and if it is decreed that I should go down because of this speech, then let me go down linked with the truth."

To the replies of his critics that he had overthrown his chances of victory and had ruined the opportunities of his party he said, "If I had to draw a pen across my record and erase my whole life from sight, and I had one poor gift or choice left as to what I should save from the wreck, I should choose that speech and leave it to the world unerased."

Riding at one time through a Virginia wood, he made the following observation about a lux-

AT THE WHITE HOUSE

uriant vine which wrapped itself about a tree: "Yes, that is very beautiful; but that vine is like certain habits of men; it decorates the ruin it makes." Speaking of the difference between character and reputation, he said: "Character was like a tree, and reputation like its shadow. The shadow is what we think of it; the tree was the real thing."

"Friday, *Feb. 19, 1864.*—As I went into the Cabinet meeting, a fair, plump lady came forward and insisted she must see the President only for a moment—wanted nothing. I made her request known to the President, who directed that she be admitted. She said her name was Holmes, that she belonged in Dubuque, Iowa, was passing East, and came from Baltimore expressly to have a look at President Lincoln. 'Well, in the matter of looking at one another,' said the President, laughing, 'I have altogether the advantage.'"—*Diary of Gideon Welles.*

Here is an incident told by Arnold that illustrates the kindly disposition of Lincoln. One summer's day, walking along the shaded path leading from the Executive Mansion to the War Office, I saw the tall, awkward form of the President seated on the grass under a tree. A wounded soldier, seeking back-pay and a pension, had met the President, and, having recognized him, asked his counsel. Lincoln sat down, examined the papers of the soldier, and told him what to do—sent him to the proper bureau with a note which secured prompt attention.

The simplicity and democracy of the lives of the President and Mrs. Lincoln may be well illustrated by the following anecdotes:

They lived their lives simply, and their servants followed the free and easy examples set before them. One of them once interrupted an important conference by opening the President's door and saying, "She wants you." "Yes, yes," Lincoln replied, without showing the least sign of annoyance. But as the President did not appear, the servant again broke in, and with greater emphasis repeated, "I say, she wants you."

Another instance indicating their freedom from ritual of all kinds is the following. A man once called on Sunday morning by appointment, and, after repeatedly ringing the door-bell and receiving no response, entered the White House unannounced and walked up-stairs, looking vainly for a servant, until he finally came to the door of the President's room, at which he knocked.

AT THE WHITE HOUSE

"Oh," exclaimed Mr. Lincoln, "the boys are all out this morning."

Early in life he had formed the habit of rising with the sun. One morning at six o'clock a passer-by saw him at the White House gateway. "Good morning," the President said. "I am looking for a newsboy. When you get to the corner I wish you would send one this way."

A telegram from Philadelphia was once received, setting forth that some one had been arrested there for obtaining fifteen hundred dollars on Mr. Lincoln's name.

"What," said Mr. Lincoln, "fifteen hundred dollars on my name! I have given no one authority for such a draft, and if I had," he added, half humorously, "it is surprising that any man could get the money."

"Do you remember, Mr. President, a request from a stranger a few days ago for your autograph, and that you gave it to him on a half-sheet of note-paper?" said Mr. Nicolay. "The scoundrel doubtless forged an order above your signature and has attempted to swindle somebody."

"Oh, that's the trick, is it?" said the President.

LINCOLN'S OWN STORIES

"What shall be done with him? Have you any orders to give?" inquired the Secretary.

"Well," said the President, slowly, "I don't see but that he will have to sit on the blister bench."

Some women called upon him and urged him to abolish slavery at once. This course of action was contrary to his views of political expediency, and when the speaker proceeded to tell him that he (Lincoln) had been appointed minister of the Lord and should follow the example of Deborah, he made the following reply, "Madam, have you finished?" Having received an affirmative reply, he said, "I have neither time nor disposition to enter into argument with you, and would end this discussion by suggesting for your consideration the question whether, if it be true that the Lord has appointed me to do the work you have indicated, it is not probable He would have communicated knowledge of that fact to me as well as to you."

When, in 1863, Maryland was carried by the Emancipationists, and the legislature adopted a resolution creating a convention that should embody a law providing for a policy of emancipation, and the convention was elected by a major-

AT THE WHITE HOUSE

ity of thirteen, there was great jubilation in Washington, and a body of Marylanders called on the President to congratulate him and the country upon the enlistment of Maryland among the free States. Lincoln made a short speech, and later on said in private: "I would rather have Maryland upon that issue than have a State twice its size upon the Presidential issue. It cleans up a piece of ground." Any one who has had any experience with cleaning up a piece of ground, digging up the roots and stumps as Lincoln had, will appreciate the simile.

What is believed to be a new story of President Lincoln is told by Adlai E. Stevenson:

"Several months before President Lincoln issued the great Proclamation of Emancipation which gave freedom to the whole race of negro slaves in America, my friend, Senator Henderson of Missouri, came to the White House one day and found Mr. Lincoln in a mood of deepest depression. Finally the great President said to his caller and friend that the most constant and acute pressure was being brought upon him by the leaders of the radical element of his party to free the slaves.

"'Sumner and Stevens and Wilson simply haunt me,' declared Mr. Lincoln, 'with their importunities for a proclamation of emancipation. Wherever I go and whatever way I turn, they are on my trail. And still, in my heart, I have the deep conviction that the hour has not yet come.'

"Just as he said this he walked to the window looking out upon Pennsylvania Avenue and stood there in silence, his tall figure silhouetted against the light of the window-pane, every line of it and of his gracious face expressive of unutterable sadness. Suddenly his lips began to twitch into a smile and his somber eyes lighted with a twinkle of something like mirth.

"'The only schooling I ever had, Henderson,' he remarked, 'was in a log school-house when reading-books and grammars were unknown. All our reading was done from the Scriptures, and we stood up in a long line and read in turn from the Bible. Our lesson one day was the story of the faithful Israelites who were thrown into the fiery furnace and delivered by the hand of the Lord without so much as the smell of fire upon their garments. It fell to one little fellow to read the verse in which occurred, for the first time in the chapter, the names of Shadrach, Meshach, and Abed-nego. Little Bud stumbled on Shadrach, floundered on Meshach, and went all to pieces on Abed-nego. Instantly the hand of the master dealt him a cuff on the side of the

AT THE WHITE HOUSE

head and left him wailing and blubbering as the next boy in line took up the reading. But before the girl at the end of the line had done reading he had subsided into sniffles, and finally became quiet. His blunder and disgrace were forgotten by the others of the class until his turn was approaching to read again. Then, like a thunderclap out of a clear sky, he set up a wail which even alarmed the master, who with rather unusual gentleness inquired:

"'"What's the matter now?"'

"'Pointing with a shaking finger at the verse which a few moments later would fall to him to read, Bud managed to quaver out the answer:

"'"Look there, marster—there comes them same damn three fellers again."'

"Then his whole face lighted with such a smile as only Lincoln could give, and he beckoned Senator Henderson to his side, silently pointing his long, bony finger to three men who were at that moment crossing Pennsylvania Avenue toward the door of the White House. They were Sumner, Wilson, and Thaddeus Stevens."

Once when a deputation visited him and urged emancipation before he was ready, he argued that he could not enforce it, and, to illustrate, asked them:

"How many legs will a sheep have if you call the tail a leg?" They answered, "Five." "You are mistaken," said Lincoln, "for calling a tail a leg don't make it so"; and that exhibited the fallacy of their position more than twenty syllogisms.

"I would save the Union," he wrote to Horace Greeley. "I would save it in the shortest way under the Constitution. If there be those who would not save the Union unless they could at the same time save slavery, I do not agree with them. If there be those who would not save the Union unless they could, at the same time, destroy slavery, I do not agree with them. My paramount object in this struggle is to save the Union, and is not either to save or destroy slavery. If I could save the Union without freeing any slave, I would do it; and if I could do it by freeing all the slaves, I would do it; and if I could save it by freeing some and leaving others alone, I would also do that. What I do about slavery and the colored race, I do because I believe it helps to save the Union; and what I forbear, I forbear because I do not believe it would help to save the Union. I shall do less whenever I believe what I am doing hurts the cause, and I shall do more whenever I believe doing more will

AT THE WHITE HOUSE

help the cause. I shall try to correct errors when shown to be errors, and I shall adopt new views as fast as they shall appear to be true views."

It may not be amiss, in a collection of this character, in order to show the marvelous fertility of this wonderful genius, to include an excerpt from his second inaugural address. This has been justly placed among the masterpieces of the world's greatest oratory. It has been compared most favorably with the loftiest portions of the Old Testament and properly classed among the most famous of all the written and spoken compositions in the English tongue. Like all of Lincoln's compositions, it had great brevity, but much pith and meat.

"Fondly do we hope, fervently do we pray, that this mighty scourge of war may speedily pass away. Yet, if God wills that it continue until all the wealth piled by the bondman's two hundred and fifty years of unrequited toil shall be sunk, and until every drop of blood drawn with the lash shall be paid by another drawn with the sword, as was said three thousand years ago, so still it must be said, 'The judgments of the Lord are true and righteous altogether.'

"With malice toward none, with charity for all, with firmness in the right, as God gives us to see the right, let us strive on to finish the work we are in; to bind up the nation's wounds; to care for him who shall have borne the battle, and for his widow and his orphan—to do all which may achieve and cherish a just and lasting peace among ourselves, and with all nations."

That Lincoln's philosophy was too shrewd and sane for him to countenance the effect rising up against the cause is proved anew by the following story from the Boston *Post*. The Hon. Alexander H. Rice once paid a visit to President Lincoln on behalf of a Boston boy who had been imprisoned for robbing his employer's letters.

After reading the petition, signed by many citizens of Boston, the President stretched himself in his chair, and asked Mr. Rice if he had met a man going down-stairs.

"Yes, Mr. President," replied Mr. Rice.

"His errand," said the President, "was to get a man pardoned out of the penitentiary; and now you have come to get a boy out of jail."

Then, with characteristic humor, Mr. Lincoln continued: "I'll tell you what it is, we must abolish these courts, or they will be the death of us. I thought it bad enough that they put so many men in the penitentiary for me to get out; but if they have now begun on the boys and the jails, and have roped you into the delivery, let's after them!

"They deserve the worst fate," he went on, "because, according to the evidence that comes to me, they pick out the very best men and send them to the penitentiary; and this present petition shows they are playing the same game on the boys and sending them all to jail.

"The man that you met on the stairs affirmed that his friend in the penitentiary is a most exemplary citizen, and Massachusetts must be a happy State if her boys out of jail are as virtuous as this one appears to be who is in.

"Yes, down with the courts and deliverance to their victims, and then we can have some peace!"

This entry appears in Welles's Diary under date of May 26, 1863:

"There was a sharp controversy between Chase and Blair on the subject of the fugitive-slave law, as attempted to be executed on one Hall here, in the district. Both were earnest: Blair for executing the law, Chase for permitting the man to enter the service of the Unites States instead of being remanded into slavery. The President said that this was one of the questions that always embarrassed him. It reminded him of a man in Illinois who was in debt and terribly annoyed by a pressing creditor, until finally the debtor assumed to be crazy whenever the creditor broached the subject. 'I,' said the President, 'have on more than one occasion in this room, when beset by extremists on this question, been compelled to appear to be very mad. I think,' he continued, 'none of you will ever dispose of this subject without getting mad.'"

There was something more than humor in this—unless wisdom itself is to be regarded as a department of humor. Probably Lincoln intended to use the word "mad" here in both its dictionary sense—as meaning insane—and the American colloquial sense—as meaning angry. Slavery was legal, and the return of fugitive slaves was called for under a decision of the Supreme Court. It took a certain amount of frenzy, joined with much righteous wrath, to cut the knot. If the American nation, typified in the great war President, had not got "mad" in both ways, slavery would certainly not have been done away with when it was.

The Hon. Hugh McCulloch, Secretary of the Treasury in Lincoln's second term, was once announced with a delegation of New York bankers.

AT THE WHITE HOUSE

As the party filed into the room he preceded them, and said to the President, in a low voice:

"These gentlemen from New York have come on to see the Secretary of the Treasury about our new loan. As bankers they are obliged to hold our national securities. I can vouch for their patriotism and loyalty, for, as the good Book says, 'Where the treasure is, there will the heart be also.'"

To which Mr. Lincoln quickly replied: "There is another text, Mr. McCulloch, I remember, that might equally apply: 'Where the carcass is, there will the eagles be gathered together.'"

When Attorney-General Bates resigned in 1864, after the resignation of Postmaster-General Blair in that year, the Cabinet was left without a Southern member. A few days before the meeting of the Supreme Court, which then met in December, Mr. Lincoln sent for Titian G. Coffey, and said: "My Cabinet has shrunk up North, and I must find a Southern man. I suppose if the twelve apostles were to be chosen nowadays, the shrieks of locality would have to be heeded."

Montgomery Blair was not popular with the Union people of the North. The public distrust

LINCOLN'S OWN STORIES

is strikingly illustrated by the following anecdote from the reminiscences of Henry Ward Beecher: "There was some talk, early in 1864, of a sort of compromise with the South. Blair told the President he was satisfied that, if he could be put in communication with some of the leading men of the South in some way or other, some benefit would accrue. Lincoln had sent a delegation to meet Alexander H. Stephens, and that was all the North knew. We were all very much excited over that. The war lasted so long, and I was afraid Lincoln would be so anxious for peace, and I was afraid he would accept something that would be of advantage to the South, so I went to Washington and called upon him. 'Mr. Lincoln, I come to you to know whether the public interest will permit you to explain to me what this Southern commission means? I am in an embarrassing position as editor and do not want to step in the dark.' Well, he listened very patiently, and looked up to the ceiling for a few moments, and said, 'Well, I am almost of a mind to show you all the documents.'

"'Well, Mr. Lincoln, I should like to see them if it is proper.' He went to his little secretary and came out and handed me a little card as long as my finger and an inch wide, and on that was written:

AT THE WHITE HOUSE

" 'You will pass the bearer through the lines' (or something to that effect).

"'A. LINCOLN.'

" 'There,' he said, 'is all there is of it. Now, Blair thinks something can be done, but I don't; but I have no objection to have him try his hand. He has no authority whatever but to go and see what he can do.' "

An editorial in the New York *Tribune*, opposing Lincoln's renomination, is said to have called out from him the following story:

"A traveler on the frontier found himself out of his reckoning one night in a most inhospitable region. A terrific thunder-storm came up to add to his trouble. He floundered along until his horse at length gave out. The lightning afforded him the only clue to his way, but the peals of thunder were frightful. One bolt, which seemed to crash the earth beneath him, brought him to his knees. By no means a praying man, his petition was short and to the point: 'O Lord, if it is all the same to you, give us a little *more light and a little less noise!*' "

When the time came along in the spring of 1864 for nominations to be made for the Presidential office by the Republican party, Fremont was prominently mentioned by a few of the malcontents, and vociferousness gave color to a support that subsequent events proved he did not have. John T. Morse, Jr., in his *Life of Abraham Lincoln*, tells the following story:

"At Cleveland on the appointed day the 'mass convention' assembled, only the mass was wanting. It nominated Fremont for the Presidency and Gen. John Cochrane for the Vice-Presidency; and thus again the Constitution was ignored by these malcontents, for both these gentlemen were citizens of New York, and therefore the important delegation from that State could lawfully vote for only one of them. Really the best result which the convention achieved was that it called forth a bit of wit from the President. Some one remarked to him that, instead of the expected thousands, only about four hundred persons had assembled. He turned to the Bible which, say Nicolay and Hay, 'commonly lay on his desk,' and read the verse: 'And every one that was in distress, and every one that was in debt, and every one that was discontented, gathered themselves unto him; and he became a captain over them; and there were with him about four hundred men.'"

"There is but one contingency that can cause your defeat for a second term," one of Lincoln's

AT THE WHITE HOUSE

friends said to him in 1863, "and that is Grant's capture of Richmond and his nomination as an opposing candidate."

"Well," replied Mr. Lincoln, shrewdly, "I feel very much about that as the man felt who said he didn't want to die particularly, but if he had got to die, that was precisely the disease he would like to die of."

Colonel McClure, the Pennsylvania journalist, tells this regarding his attitude toward the candidacy of Mr. Chase for the Presidency:

"By the way," said Mr. Lincoln, "how would it do if I were to decline Chase?"

The Colonel inquired how it could be done.

"Well," replied Lincoln, "I don't know exactly how it might be done, but that reminds me of a story of two Democratic candidates for senator in 'Egypt,' Illinois, in its early political times. That section of Illinois was almost solidly Democratic, as you know, and nobody but Democrats were candidates for office. Two Democratic candidates for senator met each other in joint debate, from day to day, and gradually became more and more exasperated at each other, until their discussions were simply disgraceful wrangles, and they both became ashamed of them. They finally agreed that either should say anything he pleased about the other, and it should not be resented as an offense; and from that time on the campaign progressed without any special display of ill-temper. On election night the two candidates, who lived in the same town, were receiving their returns together; and the contest was uncomfortably close. A distant precinct in which one of the candidates confidently expected a large majority was finally reported with a majority against him. The disappointed candidate expressed a great surprise, to which the other candidate answered that he should not be surprised, as he had taken the liberty of declining him in that district, the evening before the election. He reminded the defeated candidate that he had agreed that either was free to say anything about the other, without offense; and added that, under that authority, he had gone up into that district and taken the liberty of saying that his opponent had retired from the contest; and therefore the vote of the district was changed, and the declined candidate was thus defeated.

"I think," concluded Lincoln, with one of his hearty laughs, "I had better decline Chase."

About a fortnight before the convention in 1864 Colonel McClure, to relieve Lincoln's anx-

AT THE WHITE HOUSE

iety, showed him that a majority of the delegates were for him:

"'Well, McClure,' he replied, 'what you say seems unanswerable, but I don't quite forget that I was nominated for President in a convention that was two-thirds for the other fellow.'

"The convention came on; he was unanimously renominated. A short time after the convention, I returned to Washington. When I called to see the President, and was shown in, I saw at once a twinkle in his eye, and as I approached him he said, 'Colonel, do you remember that you told me, when here before, that everybody about Congress seemed to be against me?' I replied that I did. He said that that situation reminded him of two Irishmen who came to America and started out through the country on foot to secure work. They came to some woods, and as they passed along they heard a strange noise. They did not know what it was. So they hunted about, but could find nothing. Finally, one said to the other, 'Pat! Pat! Let's go on; this thing is nothing but a damned noise.' Lincoln said that the opposition to him was nothing but a noise."

He displayed no spirit of malice toward those who opposed his re-election. "I am in favor of short statutes of limitations in politics."

A caller upon the President on New Year's Day, 1864 said:

"I hope, Mr. President, one year from to-day I may have the pleasure of congratulating you on three events which now seem probable."

"What are they?" inquired he.

"First, that the Rebellion may be entirely crushed; second, that the constitutional amendment abolishing and prohibiting slavery may have been adopted; third, and that Abraham Lincoln may have been elected President."

"I think," replied he, with a smile, "I would be glad to accept the first two as a compromise."

When he heard that a general who was supporting McClellan had been relieved of his command the President countermanded the order, saying, "Supporting General McClellan for the Presidency is no violation of army regulations, and as a question of taste in choosing between him and me—well, I'm the longest, but he's better-looking."

Upon being congratulated on his renomination, he said, "I do not allow myself to suppose that either the Convention or the League has concluded that I am either the greatest or the best man in America, but rather they have concluded it is not best to swap horses while crossing the

AT THE WHITE HOUSE

river, and have further concluded that I am not so poor a horse that they might not make a botch of it in trying to swap." Thus arose a maxim that has since become a part of the common speech.

After a week at the Democratic Convention of 1864 a gentleman from New York called upon the President, in company with the Assistant Secretary of War, Mr. Dana. In course of conversation the gentleman said, "What do you think, Mr. President, is the reason General McClellan does not reply to the letter from the Chicago Convention?" "Oh!" replied Mr. Lincoln, with a characteristic twinkle of his eye, "he is intrenching!"

Another gentle and sympathetic speech is the one he made as he was leaving the War Department at midnight of November 10, 1864, on his re-election:

"So long as I have been here I have not willingly planted a thorn in any man's bosom. While I am deeply sensible of the high compliment of re-election, and duly grateful, as I trust, to Almighty God for having directed my countrymen to a right conclusion, as I think for their own good, it adds nothing to my satisfaction that any other man may be disappointed or pained by the result. May I ask those who have not differed from me to join with me in this same spirit toward those that have?"

Mr. Lincoln was fond of riding on horseback in the early evening to the Soldiers' Home. One night, during the latter part of 1863, he rode out with an orderly. When part way he sent the orderly back for something which he had left at the White House and rode on alone. After dusk he galloped up to the Home stables, and the hostler noticed that he was without his hat. Mr. Lincoln, answering the hostler's question, said, "Run back a few hundred yards and pick it up." The man had heard a shot, but thought little of it till Mr. Lincoln came galloping in. He found the hat and brought it to the President, who was still waiting at the stable. There was a bullet-hole near the top. Mr. Lincoln made the man promise not to speak of it. "It was probably an accident, and might worry my family." And he went to the Soldiers' Home as usual, but probably never again alone. A man had really undertaken to shoot him.

You see in this incident, and in a great many others that can be recalled, the simple, straightforward courage of the man. It never failed him.

AT THE WHITE HOUSE

The President's letters and telegrams to his wife when she and Tad were absent from Washington were almost always laden with some piece of information for Tad's special benefit. In one such communication he noted that Nanny was found resting herself and chewing her little cud on the middle of Tad's bed, and again he sent this message by telegraph, "Tell Tad the goats and father are very well, especially the goats." Perhaps the strangest document in all the volumes of the complete works of Abraham Lincoln is a telegram in reference to Tad, and sent to his wife: "Think you had better put Tad's pistol away. I had an ugly dream about him. A. L."

A few days before the President's death Secretary Stanton tendered his resignation of the War Department. He accompanied the act with a most heartfelt tribute to Mr. Lincoln's constant friendship and faithful devotion to the country, saying, also, that he, as Secretary, had accepted the position to hold it only until the war should end, and now he felt his work was done, and his duty was to resign. Mr. Lincoln was greatly moved by the Secretary's words, and, tearing in pieces the paper containing the resignation and throwing his arms about the Secretary, he said,

LINCOLN'S OWN STORIES

"Stanton, you have been a good friend and a faithful public servant, and it is not for you to say when you will no longer be needed here." Several friends of both parties were present on the occasion, and there was not a dry eye that witnessed the scene.

"The last time I saw Mr. Lincoln to speak with him," said Mr. Dana, "was in the afternoon of the day of his murder. I had received a report from the provost-marshal of Portland, Maine, saying that Jacob Thompson [a Confederate agent] was to be in that town that night for the purpose of taking the steamer for Liverpool, and what orders had the Department to give? I carried the telegram to Mr. Stanton. He said promptly, 'Arrest him'; but as I was leaving his room he called me back, adding, 'You had better take it over to the President.' It was now between four and five o'clock in the afternoon, and business at the White House was completed for the day. I found Mr. Lincoln with his coat off, in a closet attached to his office, washing his hands. 'Hello, Dana,' said he, as I opened the door, 'what is it now?' 'Well, sir,' I said, 'here is the provost-marshal of Portland, who reports that Jacob Thompson is to be in that town to-night, and

AT THE WHITE HOUSE

inquires what orders we have to give.' 'What does Stanton say?' he asked. 'Arrest him,' I replied. 'Well,' he continued, drawling his words, 'I rather guess not. When you have an elephant by the hind foot, and he wants to run away, better let him run.'"

When the Civil War was practically over Mr. Lincoln responded at once by an improvement in health and spirits, but he did not want to go to the theater on that fatal night, and not from any presentiment of evil. The play was "Our American Cousin," and he had seen it once. It was funny enough, and Mr. Lincoln loved funny things, but not twice in the same place, even for company's sake. He tried to get out of going, but Mrs. Lincoln would not permit it. She had had troubles of her own with that theater party from outside—General and Mrs. Grant having been called away at the last minute—and she did not propose to have her own husband desert her. She insisted on his going.

"All right," he said, in his meek, submissive way, when he found resistance was useless, "all right, Mary, I'll go; but if I don't go down to history as the martyr President I miss my guess."

He didn't miss his guess, but his little joke became a world tragedy.

Part V
AT THE FRONT

V

AT THE FRONT

PRESIDENT LINCOLN once said to a regiment which he was reviewing: "I happen temporarily to occupy this big White House. I am a living witness that any one of your children may look to come here as my father's child has. It is in order that each one of you may have through this free government which we have enjoyed an open field and a fair chance . . . that the struggle should be maintained, that we may not lose our birthright."

General Horace Porter is the authority for this story:

There was an officer cleaning his sword at the camp-fire when the President was visiting the camp. Mr. Lincoln came up, looked at it, took it in his hand, and said: "That is a formidable weapon, but it don't look half as dangerous to me as once did a Kentucky bowie-knife. One night I passed through the outskirts of Louisville, when suddenly a man sprang from a dark alley and drew out a bowie-knife. It looked three times as long as that sword, though I don't suppose it really was. He flourished it in front of me. It glistened in the moonlight, and for several seconds he seemed to try to see how near he could come to cutting off my nose without doing it. Finally he said, 'Can you lend me five dollars on that?' I never reached in my pockets for money so quick in the whole course of my life. Handing him a bill, I said: 'There's ten dollars, neighbor. Now put up your scythe.'"

Speaking to General Butler about the historical fact that every place that General Grant had ever taken had been held, never yielded up, Mr. Lincoln said, "When General Grant once gets possessed of a place he seems to hang on to it as if he had inherited it."

After the colored troops had been successful in making an assault, Lincoln once remarked: "I am glad the black boys have done well. I must go out and see them." He rode out with General Grant and staff, and the word was passed along the colored troops that the President was coming; then the cry arose everywhere, "Thar's

AT THE FRONT

Massa Linkum," and "Ole Fader Abraham is a-comin'," and they shouted, cheered, laughed, got down on their knees and prayed, fondled his horse, and some rushed off to tell their comrades that they had even kissed the hem of his garment. Mr. Lincoln was very much affected; he had his hat off, the tears were in his eyes, and his voice was so choked with emotion that he could scarcely respond to the salutations. It was a memorable sight to see the liberated paying their homage to the Liberator. He remarked on the way back to the camp: "When we were enlisting the colored troops there was great opposition to it, but I said to some of my critics one day, 'Well, as long as we are trying to send every able-bodied man to the front to save this country, I guess we had all better be a little color-blind. I can express my satisfaction with what they have accomplished down here something as an old-time abolitionist did upon another occasion in Illinois. He went to Chicago, and his friends took him to see Forrest play Othello. He didn't know it was a white man blacked up for the purpose, and after the play was over said, 'Well, all sectional prejudice aside, and making due allowance for my partiality for the race, darn me if I don't think the nigger held his own with any on 'em.'"

LINCOLN'S OWN STORIES

Meeting General Sheridan for the first time, he said, "General Sheridan, when this peculiar war began I thought a cavalryman should be at least six feet four inches high." But still holding Sheridan's hand in his earnest grasp and looking down on the little General, he added, "I have changed my mind—five feet four will do in a pinch." Sheridan measured five feet four and a half.

One day the President and the Secretary of State, accompanied by a young staff-officer, attended a review near Arlington, on the opposite side of the Potomac. An ambulance drawn by four mules was provided. When the party arrived on the Virginia side of the river, where the roads were rough and badly cut by artillery and army trains, the driver had so much difficulty with the team in his efforts to prevent the wheels from dropping into the ruts that he lost his temper and began to swear; the worse the road became, the greater became his profanity. At last the President said, in his pleasant manner, "Driver, my friend, are you an Episcopalian?"

Greatly astonished, the man made answer: "No, Mr. President, I ain't much of anything. But if I go to church at all I go to the Methodist church."

AT THE FRONT

"Oh, excuse me," replied Lincoln, with a smile and a twinkle in his eye; "I thought you must be an Episcopalian, for you swear just like Secretary Seward, and he is a churchwarden."

President Lincoln described Sheridan as "a little chap with round head, red face, legs longer than his body, and not enough neck to hang him by." And Colonel Ellsworth he described as "the greatest little man I ever met."

Mr. Lincoln was an unusually tall man, six feet four. Meeting a soldier considerably taller than himself, he looked him over with wondering admiration. "Say, friend," he said, "does your head know when your feet are cold?"

Upon one occasion Lincoln and Seward called at the headquarters of General McClellan and were informed that the General was out. After waiting for nearly an hour McClellan returned. Regardless of the orderly who informed him that the President and Secretary Seward were waiting, he went directly up-stairs. Mr. Lincoln, thinking that he had not been informed of his presence, sent word to him, but the information was returned that the General had retired. This discourteous act made no alteration in the President's attitude, but thereafter all conferences were held at the White House. At another time it was arranged that McClellan, Ormsby M. Mitchell, and Governor Dennison should meet at the Executive Mansion. All were on hand save the inflated General. After a long wait the gentlemen showed considerable irritation, but Mr. Lincoln said very generously:

"Never mind; I will hold McClellan's horse, if he will only bring us success."

Shortly after Antietam, owing to McClellan's inaction, the President visited the camp with his friend, O. M. Hatch, of Illinois. As they stood on the summit of a near-by hill overlooking the encampment, Mr. Lincoln said:

"Hatch, Hatch, what is all this?"

"Why," answered Mr. Hatch, "that is the Army of the Potomac."

"No, Hatch, no," said the President; "that is General McClellan's body-guard."

Usually after a defeat the President would visit the soldiers and address to them words of comfort and cheer. Sherman, upon one of these occasions, asked him to discourage cheering and all other noisy demonstrations, to which suggestion the President cheerfully assented. Sherman says

AT THE FRONT

that he made "one of the neatest, best, and most feeling addresses I ever listened to." When the boys wanted to cheer he warned them good-naturedly: "Don't cheer, boys. I confess I like it myself, but Colonel Sherman here says it is not military, and I guess we had better defer to his opinion."

A trip to the battle-field of Antietam served to accentuate certain malicious stories about the President, and Lamon urged him to deny their truthfulness. "No," said Lincoln; "in politics every man must skin his own skunk. These fellows are welcome to the hide of this one."

In the spring of 1862 the President spent several days at Fortress Monroe, awaiting military operations upon the Peninsula. As a portion of the Cabinet were with him, that was temporarily the seat of government, and he bore with him constantly the burden of public affairs. His favorite diversion was reading Shakespeare, whom he rendered with fine discrimination and feeling. One day (it chanced to be the day before the taking of Norfolk), as he sat reading alone, he called to his aide in the adjoining room, "You have been writing long enough, Colonel; come here; I want to read to you a passage in

'Hamlet.'" He read the discussion on ambition between Hamlet and his courtiers, and the soliloquy in which conscience debates of a future state. This was followed by passages from "Macbeth". Then, opening to "King John," he read from the third act the passage in which Constance bewails her imprisoned lost boy.

Then, closing the book, and recalling the words:

"And, Father Cardinal, I have heard you say
That we shall see and know our friends in heaven:
If that be true, I shall see my boy again."

Mr. Lincoln said: "Colonel, did you ever dream of a lost friend, and feel that you were holding sweet communion with that friend, and yet have a sad consciousness that it was not a reality? Just so I dream of my boy Willie." Overcome with emotion, he dropped his head on the table, and sobbed aloud.

Lincoln never forgot a point. A sentinel who was pacing near a camp-fire while Lincoln was visiting the field, listening to the stories he told, made the philosophical remark that that man had a mighty powerful memory but an awful poor "forgettery." He did not tell a story for the sake of an anecdote, but to point a moral, to clinch a fact. As an illustration of this General

AT THE FRONT

Horace Porter tells the following story, which he heard the last time he talked with Lincoln:

"We were discussing the subject of England's assistance to the South, and how, after the collapse of the Confederacy, England would find she had aided it but little and only injured herself. He said: 'That reminds me of a barber in Sangamon County. He had just gone to bed, when a stranger came along and said he must be shaved; that he had four days' beard on his face and was going to a ball, and that the beard must come off. Well, the barber reluctantly got up and dressed, and seated the man in a chair with a back so low that every time he bore down on him he came near dislocating his victim's neck. He began by lathering his face, including his nose, eyes, and ears, stropped his razor on his boot, and then made a drive at the man's countenance as if he had practised mowing in a stubble-field. He made a bold swath across the cheek, carrying away the beard, a pimple, and two warts. The man in the chair ventured the remark, "You appear to make everything level as you go." Said the barber, "Yes, and if this handle don't break, I guess I'll get away with what there is there." The man's cheeks were so hollow that the barber could not get down into the valleys with the razor, and the ingenious idea occurred to him to stick his finger in the man's mouth and press out the cheeks. Finally he cut clear through the cheek and into his own finger. He pulled the finger out of the man's mouth, snapped the blood off it, glared at him and said, "There, you lantern-jawed cuss, you've made me cut my finger."'

"'Now,' said Mr. Lincoln, 'England will find that she has got the South into a pretty bad scrape by trying to administer to her, and in the end she will find that she has only cut her own finger.'"

All through the war it was suggested that the difficulties between the North and the South could be speedily adjusted by arbitration, and numerous committees were formed, by the North especially, to meet the overtures of some committees that were formed in the South. On one occasion Mr. Lincoln reluctantly consented to be one of a committee. He recognized the absurdity of the undertaking, and knew that no committees could patch up these differences; they were too deep-rooted. At this meeting one of the Confederate committee, to illustrate a point, referred to the correspondence between King Charles the First and his Parliament, as a reliable precedent of a constitutional ruler dealing with rebels. Mr. Lincoln replied as follows: "Upon questions of history I must refer you to Mr. Seward, for he is posted in such things, and I don't profess to be; but my only distinct recollection of the matter is that *Charles lost his head!*"

Further on during the same conference one of the Confederates again pointed out the difficulties that would arise if the slaves were suddenly liberated, and would precipitate not only themselves but the entire society of the South into irremediable ruin. No work would be done, and the blacks and whites would starve together. The President waited for Mr. Seward to answer the argument, but, as that gentleman hesitated, he said:

"Mr. Hunter, you ought to know a great deal better about this matter than I, for you have always lived under the slave system. I can only say, in reply to your statement of the case, that it reminds me of a man out in Illinois, by the name of Chase, who undertook, a few years ago, to raise a very large herd of hogs. It was a great trouble to feed them, and how to get around this was a puzzle to him. At length he hit upon the plan of planting an immense field of potatoes; and, when they were sufficiently grown, he turned the whole herd into the field and let them have full swing, thus saving not only the labor of feeding the hogs, but that also of digging the potatoes. Charmed with his sagacity, he stood one day leaning against the fence, counting his hogs, when a neighbor came along.

" 'Well, well,' said he, 'Mr. Chase, this is all very fine. Your hogs are doing very well just now; but you know out here in Illinois the frost comes early, and the ground freezes a foot deep. Then what are they going to do?'

"This was a view of the matter which Mr. Chase had not taken into account. Butchering time for hogs was away on in December or January. He scratched his head, and at length stammered: 'Well, it may come pretty hard on their snouts; but I don't see but it will be root, hog, or die!' "

The commissioners, one of them being Alexander H. Stephens, who when in good health weighed about ninety pounds, dined with the President and General Grant. After dinner, as they were leaving, Stephens put on an English ulster the tails of which reached the ground, while the collar was somewhat above the wearer's head.

AT THE FRONT

As Stephens went out, Lincoln touched Grant and said: "Grant, look at Stephens. Did you ever see such a little nubbin with as much shuck?"

At the Hampton Roads conference Stephens requested that Mr. Lincoln send back his nephew, Lieutenant Stephens, who had been in a Federal prison, having been taken prisoner at Vicksburg. Mr. Lincoln sent for him.

"I told your uncle that I would send you to him, Lieutenant. You have the freedom of the city," Mr. Lincoln continued, "as long as you please to remain here. When you want to go home, let me know, and I will pass you through the lines." The interview was a memorable one, and the Lieutenant remained in Washington about two weeks, deeply moved by Lincoln's kindness. He then got a pass from the President, and at the same time Mr. Lincoln handed him his photograph, saying: "You had better take that along. It is considered quite a curiosity down your way, I believe."

After this conference, when the Confederate commissioners—Vice-President Stephens, Campbell, and Hunter—had traversed the field of official routine with Mr. Lincoln and Mr. Seward, Lincoln took the "slim, pale-faced, consump-

LINCOLN'S OWN STORIES

tive man" aside and, pointing to a sheet of paper he held in his hand, said, "Stephens, let me write 'Union' at the top of that page, and you may write below it whatever you please."

Stephens told the President that he was there to treat only on the basis of autonomy. "In that case, Stephens," said Lincoln, sadly, "I am guiltless of every drop of blood that may be shed from this onward."

Lincoln used to say, and insisted, that American humor was marked by grimness and grotesqueness, and told these stories to illustrate his viewpoint. There was a soldier in the Army of the Potomac carried to the rear of battle with both legs shot off, who, seeing a pie-woman hovering about, asked, "Say, old lady, are them pies sewed or pegged?" And there was another soldier at Chancellorsville whose regiment, waiting to be called into battle, was drinking coffee. He was about to put his mug to his lips when a stray bullet, just missing the coffee-drinker's head, dashed the mug into fragments and left the handle on his finger. The soldier angrily growled, "Johnny, you can't do that again!"

"It seems," said Lincoln, "as if neither death nor danger could quench the grim humor of the American soldier."

AT THE FRONT

On a narrow cot, in the military hospital at City Point, Major Charles H. Houghton was dying. He had been in command of Fort Haskell, a strategic point in the rear of Grant's lines, against which all the fury of Lee's attack was being directed in an effort to break the Union lines. Against Major Houghton, a mere boy of twenty years, were pitted the science and strategic knowledge of Gen. John B. Gordon, of Georgia.

Help came at last. The long-haired gray men were beaten back, and Lee's desperate move was checked. Houghton's leg was amputated and he was taken to the hospital at City Point, so that he could die in comparative peace, on a clean white cot. But for days he lingered on the borderland of life.

Sometimes in the long stretches of the night, when life and resistance are at low ebb, it seemed to those who watched that he must be zigzagging back and forth across and across that mysterious line. Yet always in the morning, when friends inquired for news of him, the surgeons could say:

"He is alive. That's all."

At nine o'clock one morning, the door at the end of the ward was opened and Dr. MacDonald, chief surgeon, called:

LINCOLN'S OWN STORIES

"Attention! The President of the United States."

There, outside the door, the sunlight streaming into the room over square, gaunt shoulders, stood Abraham Lincoln. Into the room he stalked, bending his awkward form ungracefully—for the doorway was low. At cot after cot he paused to speak some word of cheer, some message of comfort to a wounded soldier.

At Houghton's cot the two men paused. "This is the man," whispered MacDonald.

"So young!" questioned the President. "This the man that held Fort Haskell?"

MacDonald nodded.

With a large, uncouth hand the President motioned for a chair. Silently a nurse placed one at the cot's head. Houghton did not know; he could not. As though he were afraid it would clatter, and hurt the sufferer, Lincoln softly placed his "stove-pipe" hat of exaggerated fashion on the floor. Dust covered his clothes, which were not pressed. As he leaned over the cot a tawdry necktie, much awry, dangled near Houghton's head. Gently as a woman he took the wasted, colorless hand in his own sinewy one of iron strength. Just the suspicion of a pressure was there, but Houghton opened his eyes.

A smile which had forgotten suffering answered

AT THE FRONT

the great President's sad smile. In tones soft, almost musical it seemed, the President spoke to the boy on the cot, told him how he had heard of his great deeds, how he was proud of his fellow-countryman.

A few feeble words Houghton spoke in reply. At the poor, toneless voice the President winced. The doctor had told him that Houghton would die. Then happened a strange thing. The President asked to see the wound which was taking so noble a life.

Surgeons and nurses tried to dissuade him, but Lincoln insisted. The horrors of war were for him to bear as well as others, he told them, and to him the wound was a thing holy.

Bandages long and stained were removed, and the President saw.

Straightening on his feet, he flung his long, lank arms upward. A groan such as Houghton had not given voice to escaped the lips of the President.

"Oh, this war! This awful, awful war!" he sobbed.

Down the deep-lined furrows of the homely, kindly face hot tears burned their way. Slowly, tenderly, the President leaned over the pillow. The dust of travel had not been washed from his face. Now the tears, of which he was not ashamed, cut furrows in the grime and stained the white sheets on which they fell. While nurses and surgeons and men watched there in the little hospital, Abraham Lincoln took the pallid face of Houghton between his hands and kissed it just below the damp, tangled hair.

"My boy," he said, brokenly, swallowing, "you must live. You must live!"

The first gleam of real, warm, throbbing life came into the dull eyes. Houghton stiffened with a conscious, elastic tension on the cot. With a little wan smile he managed to drag a hand to his forehead. It was the nearest he could come to a salute. The awkward form of the President bent lower and lower to catch the faint, faint words.

"I intend to, sir," was what Houghton said. And he did.

Early in 1865, feeling that the downfall of the Confederacy was near, he determined to be on the scene and in readiness to meet any emergency which might arise. There he lived on a boat in the James River, opposite the cluster of huts on the bank which served as Grant's headquarters. Admiral Porter urged him to accept his bed, but he insisted upon not disturbing the Admiral and sleeping in a small state-room, whose

AT THE FRONT

berth was four inches shorter than his body. "I slept well," he said, next morning, "but you can't put a long sword in a short scabbard."

His host set carpenters to work, in the absence of his distinguished guest, to remedy the deficiency. The state-room was quickly lengthened and widened; and the following morning Lincoln soberly reported:

"A miracle happened last night; I shrank six inches in length and a foot sideways." The Admiral was positive, however, that if he had given him two fence-rails to sleep on he would not have found fault.

"Carleton," the war correspondent of the Boston *Journal*, relates the following story:

"It was during the week before Richmond was taken. The President was with General Grant and others at City Point headquarters. The party sat where they could see the river. A flatboat made its appearance, with apparently a large family on board. The President was informed that it was a planter of the vicinity, with his wife and legitimate children, and not a few colored women with their children, which were also supposed to be his own. 'Ah, yes,' said the President; 'I see. It is Abraham, Isaac, and

LINCOLN'S OWN STORIES

Ishmael, all in one boat.' The aptness of the Scriptural allusion, and the quickness of the President in responding, woke a smile on every countenance."

"I want to see Richmond," Lincoln said, when he heard that that stronghold was once more in Union hands. He went by the river from Grant's headquarters, and landed from a twelve-oared barge near Libby Prison. No military escort to meet him, and not even a vehicle of any kind. Taking his boy Tad by the hand, he walked through the streets for a mile and a half, guarded only by ten sailors. The negroes were wild with joy when they beheld their emancipator, before whom they prostrated themselves. "Don't kneel to me; that is not right," he said; and a leader among them commanded in a hoarse whisper, "'Sh—'sh—be still; heah our Saviour speak." Lincoln said: "You must kneel to God only. I am but God's humble instrument, but you may rest assured that as long as I live no one shall put a shackle on your limbs. God bless you, and let me pass on," he said to them, as he passed along. Again in the strange progress of this modest conqueror an old slave lifted his hat, and the President returned the salutation by lifting his, whereat the crowd of negroes

AT THE FRONT

who followed him gaped in wonder to see a white man uncover to a black.

Carl Schurz thus describes his entry into Richmond:

"Richmond fell. Lincoln himself entered the city on foot, accompanied only by a few officers and a squad of sailors who had rowed him ashore from the flotilla in the James River, a negro picked up on the way serving as a guide. Never had the world seen a more modest conqueror and a more characteristic triumphal procession —no army with banners and drums, only a throng of those who had been slaves, hastily run together, escorting the victorious chief into the capital of the vanquished foe. We are told that they pressed around him, kissed his hands and his garments, and shouted and danced with joy, while tears ran down the President's care-furrowed cheeks."

When he was in Richmond after it came into the possession of the Union forces, he looked for the home of George Pickett. "Is this where George Pickett lives?" he asked of a woman with a baby in her arms who answered his summons. She said she was Mrs. Pickett. Then he told her who he was, insisting that he came not as

President, but simply as "Abraham Lincoln, George's old friend." He took the little one in his arms, and thus did this noble conqueror restore the Union in one heart. He had known Pickett in Illinois and he obtained for him his appointment at West Point.

PART VI

THE COMMANDER-IN-CHIEF

VI

THE COMMANDER-IN-CHIEF

DELEGATIONS from Baltimore called to protest against the "pollution" of the soil of Maryland by the feet of the soldiers marching across it to fight against the South. They had no difficulty in understanding the President's reply:

"We must have troops; and, as they can neither crawl *under* Maryland nor fly *over* it, they must come across it."

When the war had actually begun he delighted in the soldiers' grim humor in the face of death. He told story after story about the "boys," laughing, with tears in his gray eyes, at their heroism in danger. He never laughed at the private soldier, except in the pride of his hearty patriotism. But he made constant fun of the assumptions of generals and other high officials. The stories he most enjoyed telling were of the soldiers' scoffing at rank and pretension. He delighted in the following:

LINCOLN'S OWN STORIES

A picket challenged a tug going up Broad River, South Carolina, with:

"Who goes there?"

"The Secretary of War and Major-General Foster," was the pompous reply.

"Aw! We've got major-generals enough up here—why don't you bring us up some hardtack?"

On another occasion a friend burst into his room to tell him that a brigadier-general and twelve army mules had been carried off by a Confederate raid.

"How unfortunate! Those *mules* cost us two hundred dollars apiece!" was the President's only reply.

Mr. Lincoln was a very abstemious man, ate very little and drank nothing but water, not from principle, but because he did not like wine or spirits. Once, in rather dark days early in the war, a temperance committee came to him and said that the reason we did not win was because our army drank so much whisky as to bring the curse of the Lord upon them. He said, in reply, that it was rather unfair on the part of the aforesaid curse, as the other side drank more and worse whisky than ours did.

THE COMMANDER-IN-CHIEF

Some one urged President Lincoln to place General Fremont in command of some station. While the President did not want to offend his friend at a rather critical time of the war, he pushed him gently and firmly aside in this wise: He said he did not know where to place General Fremont, and it reminded him of an old man who advised his son to take a wife, to which the young man responded, "Whose wife shall I take?"

On one occasion, exasperated at the discrepancy between the aggregate of troops forwarded to McClellan and the number of men the General reported as having received, Lincoln exclaimed, "Sending men to that army is like shoveling fleas across a barnyard—half of them never get there."

Lincoln's orders to his generals are filled with the kindly courtesy, the direct argument, and the dry humor which are so characteristic of the man. To Grant, who had telegraphed, "If the thing is pressed, I think that Lee will surrender," Lincoln replied, "Let the thing be pressed."

To McClellan, gently chiding him for his inactivity: "I have just read your despatch about sore tongue and fatigued horse. Will you par-

LINCOLN'S OWN STORIES

don me for asking what the horses of your army have done since the battle of Antietam that fatigues anything?"

Referring to General McClellan's inactivity, President Lincoln once expressed his impatience by saying, "McClellan is a pleasant and scholarly gentleman; he is an admirable engineer, but he seems to have a special talent for stationary engineering."

After a long period of inaction on the part of the Union forces a telegram from Cumberland Gap reached Mr. Lincoln, saying that firing was heard in the direction of Knoxville. The President simply remarked that he was glad of it. As General Burnside was in a perilous position in Tennessee at that time, those present were greatly surprised at Lincoln's calm view of the case. "You see," said the President, "it reminds me of Mistress Sallie Ward, a neighbor of mine, who had a very large family. Occasionally one of her numerous progeny would be heard crying in some out-of-the-way place, upon which Mrs. Ward would exclaim, 'There's one of my children not dead yet!'"

Writing to Hooker, who succeeded Burnside, Lincoln said:

THE COMMANDER-IN-CHIEF

"I believe you to be a brave and skilful soldier, which, of course, I like. I also believe you do not mix politics with your profession, in which you are right. You have confidence in yourself, which is a valuable, if not indispensable, quality. You are ambitious, which within reasonable bounds does good rather than harm; but I think that during General Burnside's command of the army you have taken counsel with your ambition, and thwarted him as much as you could, in which you did a great wrong to the country and to a most meritorious and honorable brother-officer. I have heard, in such a way as to believe it, of your recently saying that both the army and the government needed a dictator. Of course, it is not for this, but in spite of it, that I have given you the command. Only those generals who gain successes can set up dictators. What I now ask of you is military success, and I will risk the dictatorship."

General Fry, who was Provost-Marshal of the War Department and received daily instructions from the President in regard to the draft for troops, which was one of the most embarrassing and perplexing questions that arose during the war, illustrates this peculiar trait by an anecdote. He says:

LINCOLN'S OWN STORIES

"Upon one occasion the Governor of a State came to my office bristling with complaints in relation to the number of troops required from his State, the details of drafting the men, and the plan of compulsory service in general. I found it impossible to satisfy his demands, and accompanied him to the Secretary of War's office, whence, after a stormy interview with Stanton, he went alone to press his ultimatum upon the highest authority. After I had waited anxiously for some hours, expecting important orders or decisions from the President, or at least a summons to the White House for explanation, the Governor returned, and said, with a pleasant smile, that he was going home by the next train, and merely dropping in *en route* to say good-by. Neither the business he came upon nor his interview with the President was alluded to.

"As soon as I could see Lincoln I said: 'Mr. President, I am very anxious to learn how you disposed of Governor ——. He went to your office from the War Department in a towering rage. I suppose you found it necessary to make large concessions to him, as he returned from you entirely satisfied.'

"'Oh no,' he replied, 'I did not concede anything. You know how that Illinois farmer managed the big log that lay in the middle of the

THE COMMANDER-IN-CHIEF

field? To the inquiries of his neighbors, one Sunday, he announced that he had got rid of the big log. "Got rid of it!" said they. "How did you do it? It was too big to haul out, too knotty to split, and too wet and soggy to burn; what did you do?" "Well, now, boys," replied the farmer, "if you won't divulge the secret, I'll tell you how I got rid of it. *I plowed around it.*" Now,' said Lincoln, 'don't tell anybody, but that's the way I got rid of Governor ——. *I plowed around* him, but it took me three mortal hours to do it, and I was afraid every moment he'd see what I was at.'"

Commenting on Jeb Stuart's raid into Maryland and Pennsylvania and his complete circuit of McClellan's army and his return over the river unharmed despite McClellan's attempt to head him off, Lincoln remarked:

"When I was a boy we used to play a game, three times round and out. Stuart has been round twice; if he goes round him once more, gentlemen, McClellan will be out."

The General ascribed Stuart's success to his lack of horses, and telegraphed that unless the army got more horses there would be similar expeditions. To this Halleck telegraphed:

"The President has read your telegram, and

directs me to suggest that if the enemy had more occupation south of the river his cavalry would not be so likely to make raids north of it."

"McClellan's tardiness," said Lincoln, "reminds me of a fellow in Illinois who had studied law but had never tried a case. He was sued, and, not having confidence in his ability to manage his own case, employed a lawyer to manage it for him. He had only a confused idea of the meaning of law terms, and, on the trial, constantly made suggestions to his lawyer, who paid but little attention to him. At last, fearing that his lawyer was not handling the opposing counsel very well, he lost all his patience, and, springing to his feet, cried out:

" 'Why don't you go at him with a fi. fa., a demurrer, a capias, a surrebutter, or ne exeat, or something, and not stand there like a nudum pactum or a non est?' "

A new levy of troops required, on a certain occasion, the appointment of a large additional number of brigadier and major generals. Among the immense number of applications, Mr. Lincoln came upon one wherein the claims of a certain worthy (not in the service at all) "for a generalship" were glowingly set forth. But the appli-

THE COMMANDER-IN-CHIEF

cant did not set forth whether he wanted to be a brigadier or a major general. The President observed this difficulty and solved it by a lucid indorsement. The clerk, on receiving the paper again, found written across its back, "Major-General, I reckon. A. LINCOLN."

A woman once approached the President rather imperiously. "Mr. President," she said, very theatrically, "you must give me a colonel's commission for my son. Sir, I demand it, not as a favor, but as a right. Sir, my grandfather fought at Lexington. Sir, my uncle was the only man that did not run away at Bladensburg. Sir, my father fought at New Orleans, and my husband was killed at Monterey."

"I guess, madam," answered Mr. Lincoln, dryly, "your family has done enough for the country. It is time to give somebody else a chance."

Some gentlemen were once finding fault with the President because certain generals were not given commands. "The fact is," replied Mr. Lincoln, "I've got more pegs than I have holes to put them in."

One of the telegraph operators at the War Department relates that the President came over there at night during the war and remarked that he had just been reading a little book which some one had given to his son Tad. It was a story of a motherly hen who was struggling to raise her brood and teach them to lead honest and useful lives, but in her efforts she was greatly annoyed by a mischievous fox who made sad havoc with her offspring. "I thought I would turn over to the finis and see how it came out," said the President. "This is what it said: 'And the fox became a good fox, and was appointed paymaster in the army.' I wonder who he is!"

A person who wished to be commissioned as brigadier told Mr. Lincoln in a sarcastic tone, "I see there's no vacancy among the brigadiers from the fact that so many colonels are commanding brigades."

"My friend," said Mr. Lincoln, "let me tell you something about that. You are a farmer, I believe; if not, you will understand me also. Suppose you had a large cattle-yard, full of all sorts of cattle, cows, oxen, and bulls, and you kept killing, selling, and disposing of the cows and oxen in one way or another, taking good care of the bulls; by and by you would find out that you had nothing but a yard full of old bulls, good for nothing under heaven.

THE COMMANDER-IN-CHIEF

"Now it will be just so with the army if I don't stop making brigadier-generals."

A woman came to the White House one day on an unusual errand, which the President suspected was a pretext, but he took her at her word and gave her the following note to Major Ramsey, of the quartermaster's department:

"My Dear Sir,—The lady bearer of this says she has two sons who want to work. Set them at it if possible. Wanting to work is so rare a merit that it should be encouraged.
          "A. Lincoln."

In the most trying days of the war Lincoln was strolling down Pennsylvania Avenue one evening in company with one of his old and intimate friends from Illinois. He was somewhat anxious and depressed, for there still appeared at times a strange melancholic vein in his temperament. He felt grievously the overpowering responsibility of his position, and some special care of the moment rested apprehensively upon his mind.

The two friends walked slowly along in silence, when suddenly a man stepped in front of the President, and, presenting a paper, said:

"Mr. Lincoln, this is the only opportunity I

have had to speak to you. Please consider my case. I—"

Here Mr. Lincoln interrupted him impatiently: "My man, don't annoy me this way. I have too much to think of. You must let me alone."

Then he passed on with his companion, leaving the applicant standing dejectedly on the sidewalk.

The two friends walked a short distance without speaking, when suddenly Mr. Lincoln stopped and said:

"John, I treated that man shamefully. I must go back and see him."

And he at once turned and walked up to the petitioner, who had remained in his despondent attitude.

"My friend," said Lincoln, "I was rude to you just now; I ask your pardon. I have a great deal to worry and trouble me at this time, but I had no right to treat you so uncivilly. Take this card, and come to my office in the morning, and I will do what I can for you. Good-night."

That done, he rejoined his friend, to resume his melancholy manner, and silently they walked on as before.

Noah Brookes relates the following:

"Returning from a visit to the Army of the

THE COMMANDER-IN-CHIEF

Potomac, when its depots were at City Point, I gave an account of my visit to the President, as he had sent me with a special pass to Grant's headquarters. He asked, jocularly, 'Did you meet any colonels who wanted to be brigadiers, or any brigadiers who wanted to be major-generals, or any major-generals who wanted to run things?' Receiving a reply in the negative, he stretched out his hand in mock congratulation, and said, 'Happy man!'

"Afterward an officer who had been attentive to our little party did come to my lodgings and complain that he ought to be promoted, urging, among other things, that his relationship to a distinguished general kept him down. I told the incident to the President, after recalling his previous questions to me. Lincoln fairly shrieked with laughter, and, jumping up from his seat, cried, 'Keeps him down! Keeps him down! That's all that keeps him up.'"

When Lincoln pleaded for a commission for his son Robert he pleaded for it in his own peculiar and diffident way. This communication has a peculiar interest in view of the fact that it came from one who bestowed such favors by the thousand. Writing to General Grant, he says:
"Please read and answer this letter as though

LINCOLN'S OWN STORIES

I was not President, but only a friend. My son, now in his twenty-second year, having graduated at Harvard, wishes to see something of the war before it ends. I do not wish to put him in the ranks, nor yet give him a commission to which those who have already served long are better entitled and better qualified to hold.

"Could he, without embarrassment to you or detriment to the service, go into your military family with some nominal rank, I, and not the public, furnishing his necessary means? If not, say so without the least hesitation, because I am as anxious and as deeply interested that you shall not be encumbered as you can be yourself."

Once upon learning that a woman he had seen in the halls of the War Department was there for the purpose of securing a pass to visit her husband in the Army of the Potomac, which was against the rules, in order to show him their first-born, Lincoln did not rest until he had telegraphed for the husband to come to Washington, and a bed had been assigned to the mother and child in one of the Washington hospitals.

His gentleness is also exhibited in the following incident related by Morgan. He once reproved a man who had been refused by every one else

THE COMMANDER-IN-CHIEF

for following him to the Soldiers' Home, his only refuge, and sent him away. Next day, after a night of remorse, he sought the man out at his hotel, and begged his forgiveness for treating "with rudeness one who had offered his life for his country" and was in trouble. Taking him into his carriage, the President got him out of his troubles. When he told Stanton what he had done, the grim Secretary himself apologized for rejecting the appeal.

"No, no," said Lincoln, "you did right in adhering to your rules. If we had such a soft-hearted fool as I am in your place, there would be no rules that the army or the country could depend on."

This story shows his accessibility and friendliness and the humorous disposition which was so characteristic with him. A tax had been levied on oxen. An owner of a pair came to Lincoln, who had more on his shoulders than any other man in the world, to see if he would not help him to get rid of the tax. Lincoln knew the man, and remembered the oxen, and said: "Are those the oxen I see standing at the corner whenever I go to the Treasury? I never saw them move. Maybe they are not movable property. Perhaps we may get them put down as real estate." In this incident Lincoln appears in a patriarchal character, which was certainly his, reminding us of an Oriental prince seated at the gate of his palace, or rather the representation of one in comic opera.

A year or more before Mr. Lincoln's death a delegation of clergymen waited upon him in reference to the appointment of the army chaplains. The delegation consisted of a Presbyterian, a Baptist, and an Episcopal clergyman. They stated that the character of many of the chaplains was notoriously bad, and they had come to urge upon the President the necessity of more discretion in these appointments.

"But, gentlemen," said the President, "that is a matter which the Government has nothing to do with; the chaplains are chosen by the regiments."

Not satisfied with this, the clergymen pressed, in turn, a change in the system. Mr. Lincoln heard them through without remark, and then said, "Without any disrespect, gentlemen, I will tell you a little story.

"Once, in Springfield, I was going off on a short journey, and reached the depot a little ahead of time. Leaning against the fence just outside the depot was a little darky boy whom

THE COMMANDER-IN-CHIEF

I knew, named Dick, busily digging with his toe in a mud-puddle. As I came up I said, 'Dick, what are you about?'

"'Making a *church*,' said he.

"'A church!' said I; 'what do you mean?'

"'Yes, yes,' said Dick, pointing with his toe; 'don't you see? There is the shape of it; there's the steps and front door—here the pews, where the folks set, and there's a pulpit.'

"'Yes, I see,' said I, 'but why don't you make a minister?'

"'Laws,' answered Dick, with a grin, 'I hain't got *mud* enough!'"

In the course of the Rebellion an Austrian count applied to President Lincoln for a position in the army. Being introduced by the Austrian minister, he needed, of course, no further recommendation; but, as if fearing that his importance might not be fully appreciated, he proceeded to explain that he was a count, that his family were ancient and highly respectable, when Lincoln, with a merry twinkle in his eye, tapping the aristocratic lover of titles on the shoulder in a fatherly way, as if the man had confessed to some wrong, interrupted, in a soothing tone, "Never mind; you will be treated with just as much consideration for all that!"

LINCOLN'S OWN STORIES

A woman once requested of Lincoln that a church in Alexandria that was being used for a hospital be given up and rededicated for purposes of worship. Mr. Lincoln asked if she had applied to the post surgeon, and being assured that she had but that he could do nothing for her, Lincoln said, "Well, madam, that is an end of it then."

More for the purpose of testing her sentiments, Mr. Lincoln continued: "You say you live in Alexandria. How much would you be willing to subscribe toward building a hospital there?"

She replied: "You may be aware, Mr. Lincoln, that our property has been very much embarrassed by the war, and I could not afford to give much for such a purpose."

"Yes," said Mr. Lincoln, "and this war is not over yet; and I expect we shall have another fight soon, and that church may be very useful as a hospital in which to nurse our poor wounded soldiers. It is my candid opinion that God wants that church for our wounded fellows. So, madam, you will excuse me. I can do nothing for you."

Afterward, in speaking of this incident, Mr. Lincoln said that the lady as a representative of her class in Alexandria reminded him of a story of the young man who had an aged mother and father owning considerable property. The

THE COMMANDER-IN-CHIEF

young man, being an only son, and believing that the old people had lived out their usefulness, assassinated them both. He was accused, tried, and convicted of the murder. When the judge came to pass sentence upon him, and called upon him to give any reason he might have why the sentence of death should not be passed upon him, he with great promptness replied that he hoped the court would be lenient to him because he was a poor orphan!

"His skill in parrying troublesome questions was wonderful," said Mr. Chauncey M. Depew. "I was in Washington at a critical period of the war, when the late John Ganson, of Buffalo, one of the ablest lawyers in our State, and who, though elected as a Democrat, supported all Mr. Lincoln's war measures, called on him for explanations. Mr. Ganson was very bald, with a perfectly smooth face, and had a most direct and aggressive way of stating his views or of demanding what he thought he was entitled to. He said:

"'Mr. Lincoln, I have supported all of your measures and think I am entitled to your confidence. We are voting and acting in the dark in Congress, and I demand to know—I think I have the right to ask and to know—what is the present situation and what are the prospects and conditions of the several campaigns and armies?'

"Mr. Lincoln looked at him quizzically for a moment, and then said, 'Ganson, how clean you shave!'

"Most men would have been offended, but Ganson was too broad and intelligent a man not to see the point and retire at once, satisfied, from the field."

To a politician who criticized his course he wrote, "Would you have me drop the war where it is, or would you prosecute it in future with elder-stalk squirts charged with rose water?"

The President was once called upon in reference to a newly invented gun, concerning which a committee had been appointed to make a report.

The "report" was sent for, and when it came it was found to be of the most voluminous description. Mr. Lincoln glanced at it, and said, "I should want a new lease of life to read this through!" Throwing it down upon the table, he added: "Why can't a committee of this kind occasionally exhibit a grain of common sense? If I send a man to buy a horse for me, I expect him to tell me his *points*—not how many *hairs* there are in his tail."

THE COMMANDER-IN-CHIEF

Mr. Lincoln sometimes had a very effective way of dealing with men who troubled him with questions. A visitor once asked him how many men the rebels had in the field.

The President replied, very seriously, "*Twelve hundred thousand, according to the best authority.*"

The interrogator grew pale, and ejaculated, "Good heavens!"

"Yes, sir; twelve hundred thousand—no doubt of it. You see, all of our generals, when they get whipped, say the enemy outnumbers them from three or five to one, and I must believe them. We have four hundred thousand men in the field, and three times four make twelve. Don't you see it?"

Here is a story told by General Fisk that Mr. Lincoln relished much and often repeated.

When Fisk became a colonel he organized his regiment with the understanding that he was to do all the swearing of the regiment. One of the teamsters, however, as the roads were not always of the best, had difficulty in controlling his temper and his tongue. Once, under unusual difficulties, through a series of mud-pools a little worse than usual, unable to control himself any longer, this teamster burst forth into a volley of energetic oaths.

The Colonel took him to account and reminded him that he had agreed to let him (the Colonel) do all the swearing of the regiment.

"Yes, I did, Colonel," he replied. "But the fact was, the swearing had to be done then or not at all, and you weren't there to do it."

Being informed of the death of John Morgan, he said, "Well, I wouldn't crow over anybody's death; but I can take this as resignedly as any dispensation of Providence."

The President was once speaking about an attack made on him by the Committee on the Conduct of the War for a certain alleged blunder, or something worse, in the Southwest, the matter involved being one which had fallen directly under the observation of the officer to whom he was talking, who possessed official evidence completely upsetting all the conclusions of the committee.

"Might it not be well for me," queried the officer, "to set this matter right in a letter to some paper, stating the facts as they actually transpired?"

"Oh no," replied the President; "at least, not now. If I were to try to read, much less answer, all the attacks made on me, this shop

THE COMMANDER-IN-CHIEF

might as well be closed for any other business. I do the very best I know how—the very best I can; and I mean to keep doing so until the end. If the end brings me out all right, what is said against me won't amount to anything. If the end brings me out wrong, ten angels swearing I was right will make no difference."

"Well," said Mr. Lincoln, on a certain occasion, "I feel about that a good deal as a man whom I will call 'Jones,' whom I once knew, did about his wife. He was one of your meek men, and had the reputation of being badly henpecked. At last one day his wife was seen switching him out of the house. A day or two afterward a friend met him in the street, and said: 'Jones, I have always stood up for you, as you know; but I am not going to do it any longer. Any man who will stand quietly and take a switching from his wife deserves to be horsewhipped.' Jones looked up with a wink, patting his friend on the back. '*Now, don't,*' said he; 'why, it didn't hurt me any; and you've no idea what a *power of good* it did Sarah Ann!'"

Speaking of resentment, he said:
"Perhaps I have too little of it; but I never

thought it paid. A man has no time to spend half his life in quarrels."

Once, in reply to a delegation of bank presidents who urged whether it was not time to give up all thought of the Union, he told the following story:

"When I was a young man in Illinois I boarded for a time with the deacon of the Presbyterian church. One night I was roused from my sleep by a rap at the door, and I heard the deacon's voice exclaiming, 'Arise, Abraham! The Day of Judgment has come!' I sprang from my bed and rushed to my window, and saw stars falling in great showers; but, looking back of them in the heavens, I saw the grand old constellations, with which I was so well acquainted, fixed and true in their places. Gentlemen, the world did not come to an end then, nor will the Union now."

He could be stern at times, and when the frantic cry arose from the Northern commercial interests for compromise, he said: "They seek a sign, and none shall be given them. . . . I am not insensible to any commercial or financial depression that may exist, but nothing is to be gained by fawning around the 'respectable scoundrels' who got it up. Let them go to work to repair the mischief of their own doing, and then perhaps they will be less greedy to do the like again."

As President, Lincoln was still the same great democrat he had always been as a citizen. During the four awful years of war his heart and his thoughts were always with the soldier in the ranks—and in both ranks, for the North and the South was his country. So intent was Lincoln upon saving all unnecessary suffering that the doorkeepers had standing orders from him that, no matter how great the throng, though Senators and Representatives had to wait or to go away without an audience, the President must see before the day closed every messenger who came to him with a petition for the saving of a life.

In connection with this he once said, "Some of our generals complain that I impair discipline in the army by my pardons and respites, but it makes me rested after a hard day's work if I can find some good excuse for saving a man's life, and I go to bed happy as I think how joyous the signing of my name will make him and his family and his friends."

Upon a petition for the release of a soldier condemned to death Lincoln wrote: "What possible injury can this lad work upon the cause of the great Union? I say, let him go."

It is a lasting loss to American history that there was not a special secretary at the White House during Lincoln's administration to record the stories of all Lincoln's pardons. Think of the story that lies back of the short and simple order, "Let this woman have her boy."

In passing upon a case of a lad condemned to death for falling asleep upon his post, Lincoln said: "I could not think of going into eternity with the blood of that poor young man on my skirts. It is not to be wondered at that a boy raised on a farm, probably in the habit of going to bed at dark, should, when required to watch, fall asleep; and I cannot consent to shoot him for such an act." The impressive sequel of this act of mercy was brought to light when the dead body of this soldier boy was found on the field of Fredericksburg, and next to his heart a photograph of the President, across which he had written, "God bless Abraham Lincoln."

After pardoning a deserter (condemned to death), in answer to the prayer of his mother, Lincoln said, "Perhaps I have done wrong, but, at all events, I have made that poor woman happy."

THE COMMANDER-IN-CHIEF

Speed tells of a scene in the Presidential office that was very touching. An aged mother who had been pleading for the liberty of her boy, and whose petition had been granted, said, as she was leaving, "I shall probably never see you again until we meet in Heaven."

Speed remonstrated with Mr. Lincoln, urging that he had no business to expose himself to such nerve-racking scenes.

"Things of the sort you have just seen don't hurt me," insisted Lincoln; "it is the only thing to-day that has made me forget my condition or given me any pleasure." He added, "Die when I may, I want it said of me by those who knew me best that I plucked a thistle and planted a flower where I thought a flower would grow."

The President kept on a table near him a pile of thin blank cards on which he penciled some of his most important orders. After listening patiently to a long complaint about the harsh or unjust treatment some chaplain, soldier, or citizen had suffered, Mr. Lincoln took grim delight in writing to the Secretary of War:

"DEAR STANTON,—*Let up on* So-and-so.
"A. LINCOLN."

Once it became Lincoln's duty to give an official reprimand to a young officer who had been court-martialed for a quarrel with one of his associates. The reprimand is probably the gentlest record in the annals of penal discourses, and it shows in few words the principles which ruled the conduct of this great and peaceable man.

"The advice of a father to his son, 'Beware of entrance to a quarrel, but, being in, bear it, that the opposer may beware of thee,' is good, but not the best."

"Quarrel not at all. No man resolved to make the most of himself can spare time for personal contention. Still less can he afford to take all the consequences, including the vitiation of his temper and the loss of self-control.

"Yield larger things to which you can show no more than equal right; and yield lesser ones, though clearly your own.

"Better give your path to a dog than be bitten by him in contesting for the right. Even killing the dog would not cure the bite."

When his generals remonstrated with him for his laxity in enforcing army rules, he never could forget that after all a volunteer army was a human organization and that every soldier was a son of his. And when it is considered that of two and a half million enlistments more than

THE COMMANDER-IN-CHIEF

two million were boys under twenty-one, and that they graded all the way down to fifteen, they were indeed children.

"There are already too many weeping widows," Lincoln insisted, when objection was made because he had forbidden the shooting of twenty-four deserters in a row; "for God's sake, don't ask me to add to the number, for I won't do it."

"They are shooting a boy to-day," he once said; "I hope I have not done wrong to allow it."

"To-morrow is butcher's day," he said, one Thursday, as he was looking over a heap of sentences that lay upon his desk, "and I must go through these papers and see if I can't find some excuse to let these poor fellows off."

Appeals for clemency were made to him at all times and places. Once a man went to him late at night and aroused him from his slumbers. He sat up in his night-clothes suspending the sentence of a nineteen-year-old boy for having fallen asleep at his post. And Lincoln was so troubled lest his order might go wrong that he dressed himself and went in person to the War Department. Once when he feared that a similar order might go astray he telegraphed to four persons. Thousands of instances might be multiplied. "If he has no friend, I'll be his friend," he said, when he ordered a stay of a sentence that was to execute a soldier.

The most whimsical reason for granting a pardon was that given to a German girl, who came, poorly dressed, to plead, in broken English, for the life of her brother, who, not understanding English very well, had enlisted and deserted. The President said to her, kindly:

"I'll be whipped if I don't pardon your brother. Here you have come without an influential friend to help you—but you seem to be a good, honest girl." Then his eye fell upon her scant skirts. "Yes, I'll pardon him—because—because—*you don't wear hoops!*"

One day an old man came to him with a sad tale of sorrow. His boy had been convicted of unpardonable crimes and sentenced to death, but he was an only son; and Lincoln said, kindly:

"I am sorry I can do nothing for you. Listen to this telegram I received from General Butler yesterday:

"'PRESIDENT LINCOLN, I pray you not to interfere with the courts-martial of the army. You will destroy all discipline among our soldiers.

"'B. F. BUTLER.'"

Lincoln watched the old man's grief for a

THE COMMANDER-IN-CHIEF

minute, and then exclaimed, "By jingo! Butler or no Butler, here goes!" Writing a few words, he handed the paper to the old man, reading:

"Job Smith is not to be shot until further orders from me. ABRAHAM LINCOLN."

"Why," said the old man, sadly, "I thought it was a pardon. You may order him to be shot next week."

"My friend," replied the President, "I see you are not very well acquainted with me. If your son never dies till orders come from me to shoot him, he will live to be a great deal older than Methuselah."

A Congressman who had failed to move Secretary Stanton to grant a pardon went to the White House late at night after the President had retired, forced the way to his bedroom, and earnestly besought his interference, exclaiming earnestly:

"This man, Mr. Lincoln, must not be shot."

"Well," said the President, coolly, "I do not believe shooting will do him any good," and the pardon was granted.

One day a woman accompanied by a Senator called on the President. The woman was the wife of one of Mosby's men. Her husband had

LINCOLN'S OWN STORIES

been captured, tried, and condemned to be shot. She came to ask for his pardon. The President heard her story, and then asked what kind of man her husband was. "Is he intemperate? Does he abuse the children and beat you?" "No, no," said the wife; "he is a good man, a good husband; he loves me, and he loves the children, and we cannot live without him. The only trouble is that he is a fool about politics. I live in the North, born there, and if I get him home he will do no more fighting for the South." "Well," said Mr. Lincoln, after examining the papers, "I will pardon your husband and turn him over to you for safe keeping." The poor woman, overcome with joy, sobbed as though her heart would break.

"My dear woman," said Lincoln, "if I had known how badly it was going to make you feel, I never would have pardoned him." "You do not understand me," she cried, between her sobs— "you do not understand me." "Yes, yes, I do," answered the President; "and if you do not go away at once I shall be crying with you."

One day Judge Holt, the Judge-Advocate General of the army, in laying death-sentences before the President, came to the case of a young soldier who in battle hid behind a stump, and demoralized

THE COMMANDER-IN-CHIEF

his regiment by his cowardice. Lincoln remarked, "Well, I'll have to put that with my leg cases."

"Leg cases!" said Judge Holt. "What do you mean by leg cases, sir?"

"Why, why," replied Mr. Lincoln, "do you see those papers crowded into those pigeonholes? They are the cases that you call by that long title, 'cowardice in the face of the enemy,' but I call them, for short, my 'leg cases.' But I put it to you to decide for yourself: If Almighty God gives a man a cowardly pair of legs, how can he help their running away with him?"

Chauncey M. Depew tells the following:

The reception held by the President day by day was a series of amusing or affecting scenes. He at once satisfied and reconciled an importunate but lifelong friend who wanted a mission to a distant country where the climate was very unhealthy by saying, when all arguments failed, "Strangers die there soon, and I have already given the position to a gentleman whom I can better spare than you."

When a little woman whose scant raiment and pinched features indicated the struggle of respectability with poverty secured, after days of effort, an entrance to his presence, he said,

"Well, my good woman, what can I do for you?" She replied: "My son, my only child, is a soldier. His regiment was near enough to my house for him to take a day and run over and see his mother. He was arrested as a deserter when he re-entered the lines and condemned to be shot, and he is to be executed to-morrow." Hastily arising from his chair, the President left Senators and Congressmen and Generals, and, seizing the little woman by the hand, dragged her on a run, as with great strides he marched with her to the office of the Secretary of War. She could not tell where the regiment then was, or at what place or in what division the execution was to take place, and Stanton, who had become wearied with the President's clemency, which, he said, destroyed discipline, begged the President to drop the matter; but Mr. Lincoln, rising, said with vehemence, "I will not be balked in this. Send this message to every headquarters, every fort, and every camp in the United States: 'Let no military execution take place until further orders from me. A. LINCOLN.'"

Another instance of the many that show his gentleness and consideration is here given:

"The case of Andrews is really a very bad one, as appears by the record already before me.

THE COMMANDER-IN-CHIEF

Yet before receiving this I had ordered his punishment commuted to imprisonment with hard labor during the war, and had so telegraphed. I did this, not on any merit in the case, but because I am trying to evade the butchering business lately."

An officer had disobeyed, or failed to comprehend an order.

"I believe I'll sit down," said Secretary Stanton, "and give that man a piece of my mind."

"Do so," said Lincoln; "write him now while you have it on your mind. Make it sharp. Cut him all up."

Stanton did not need a second invitation. It was a "bone-crusher" that he read to the President.

"That's right," said Lincoln; "that's a good one."

"Whom can I send it by?" mused the Secretary.

"Send it!" replied Lincoln, "send it! Why, don't send it at all. Tear it up. You have freed your mind on the subject, and that is all that is necessary. Tear it up. You never want to send such letters. I never do."

Mr. Lincoln's language in ordinary conversation was characterized by the same simplicity which adorned his speeches.

LINCOLN'S OWN STORIES

"You never swear, Mr. President, do you?" asked a prominent Boston man, who had talked with him on several occasions.

"Oh, I don't have to," he laughed, not loud, but deep. "You know I have Stanton in my Cabinet."

This may have been a reflection upon the virile and vitriolic Secretary of War, but it was no less a delicate compliment.

One morning Mr. Lincoln met a well-preserved tramp near the White House grounds. The tramp didn't know the President, and struck him for the loan of a dime to save him from immediate starvation.

"You look like an able-bodied man," said the President; "why don't you join the army?"

"They won't let me," whined the tramp. "I'd be glad enough to die for my country, sir, if they would give me the chance."

"Well, maybe I can be of service," said Mr. Lincoln, kindly. Taking an envelop and pencil from his pocket he wrote a note and addressed it to the officer in charge of the recruiting station near by, in Fifteenth Street. "Take that," he said, passing it over, "and give it to the officer at No. 714 Fifteenth Street. If he can't do anything for you, come back here to me. I'm just walking around."

THE COMMANDER-IN-CHIEF

The tramp took it and shuffled away, but he never came back; neither did he go to the recruiting office. The note was to this effect:

"COLONEL FIELDING,—The bearer is anxious to go to the front and die for his country. Can't you give him a chance?"

An officer once forced his way into the presence of the President and said he had a grievance to lay before him against Sherman, who had threatened to shoot him.

"Well, if I were you, and he threatened to shoot, I wouldn't trust him, for I believe he would do it."

A gentleman was relating to the President how a friend of his had been driven away from New Orleans as a Unionist, and how, on his expulsion, when he asked to see the writ by which he was expelled, the deputation which called on him told him that the Government had made up their minds to do nothing illegal and so they had issued no illegal writs, and simply meant to make him go of his own free will. "Well," said Mr. Lincoln, "that reminds me of a hotel-keeper down at St. Louis who boasted that he never had a death at his hotel, for whenever a guest was dying in his house he carried him out to die in the gutter."

LINCOLN'S OWN STORIES

Once, as he drove up to a hospital, Lincoln saw one of the inmates walking directly in front of his team, and he cried out to the driver to stop. The horses were checked none too soon to avoid running the man down. Then Lincoln saw that the poor fellow, only a boy, had been shot in both eyes. He got out of his carriage, and, taking the blind soldier by the hand, asked him in trembling tones for his name, his service, and his residence. "I am Abraham Lincoln," he himself said as he was leaving, and the sightless face of the youth was lit up with gratitude as he listened to the President's words of honest sympathy. The next day the chief of the hospital laid in the boy's hands a commission as first lieutenant in the army of the United States, bearing the President's signature, and with it an order retiring him on three-quarters pay for the years of helplessness that until then had stretched before him through a hopeless future.

In 1862 the people of New York City feared bombardment by Confederate cruisers, and public meetings were held to consider the gravity of the situation. Finally a delegation of fifty gentlemen, representing hundreds of millions of dollars, was selected to go to Washington and persuade the President to detail a gunboat to protect their

THE COMMANDER-IN-CHIEF

property. David Davis, while on the Supreme Bench, went to the White House and presented them to the President.

Mr. Lincoln heard them attentively, much impressed, apparently, by the "hundreds of millions." When they had concluded, he said:

"Gentlemen, I am, by the Constitution, Commander-in-Chief of the Army and the Navy of the United States, and as a matter of law I can order anything to be done that is practicable to be done. I am in command of the gunboats and ships of war; but, as a matter of fact, I do not know exactly where they are. I presume they are actively engaged, and it is therefore impossible for me to furnish you with a gunboat. The credit of the Government is at a very low ebb, greenbacks are not worth more than forty or fifty cents on the dollar; and in this condition of things, if I were worth half as much as you gentlemen are represented to be, and as badly frightened as you seem to be, I would build a gunboat and give it to the Government."

Judge Davis said he never saw one hundred millions sink to such insignificant proportions as it did when the delegation left the White House.

When the war was still only half over, many people at the North felt that a more vigorous policy was demanded. There had been a meeting of prominent Northern men, including Governors of Northern States. They passed resolutions that the campaign should be more aggressive, and commissioned Mr. Dixon to call on Mr. Lincoln, tell him of the meeting, and read to him a record of its conclusions.

Mr. Dixon said that he undertook the task with a great deal of satisfaction, and felt like a very large-sized man when he went up to the White House one evening to deliver himself of his mission.

Mr. Lincoln listened in silence to what Mr. Dixon had to say, a silence which added not a little to the impressiveness of the latter's eloquence. When Mr. Dixon was done, Mr. Lincoln said to him:

"Dixon, you are a good fellow, and I have always had a high opinion of you. It is needless for me to add that what comes from those who sent you here is authoritative. The Governors of the Northern States are the North. What they decide must be carried out.

"Still, in justice to myself, you must remember that Abraham Lincoln is the President of the United States. Anything that the President of the United States does, right or wrong, will be the acts of Abraham Lincoln, and Abraham Lin-

THE COMMANDER-IN-CHIEF

coln will by the people be held responsible for the President's actions.

"But I have a proposition to make to you. Go home and think the matter over. Come to me to-morrow morning at nine o'clock and I will promise to do anything that you then have determined upon as right and proper. Good night."

Mr. Dixon left the White House feeling much larger than when he entered it, assured that the President put a higher value upon his abilities than he had himself supposed. Dismissing this pleasant thought, he consulted with himself as to what should be done, now that the responsibility had fallen on him to decide the policy of the President of the United States. He endeavored most seriously to put himself in the place of the President and to find the best solution for the great problems which must be met.

Many suggestions occurred to him, but one after another was dismissed as for some reason out of the question. When morning broke he had not determined upon the policy which he was to impose upon the President. He decided not to go to the White House that morning. He did not go the next day, nor the next.

Indeed, three weeks went by before he saw the President. Then it was at a reception at Secretary Seward's, and Mr. Dixon tried to get by him in the crowd without attracting special attention; but the long arm of the President shot out, seized, and dragged him to one side.

"By the way, Dixon," said Mr. Lincoln, "I believe I had an appointment with you one morning about three weeks ago." Mr. Dixon said he recalled something of the sort. "Where have you been all these weeks?" asked the President.

"Here in Washington," said Dixon; "but, to tell the truth, Mr. President, I have decided never to keep that appointment."

"I thought you would not when I made it for you," was Mr. Lincoln's comment.

His power of metaphor is well illustrated in this message to Hooker in the Gettysburg campaign: "If the head of Lee's army is at Martinsburg and the tail of it on the plank road between Fredericksburg and Chancellorsville, the animal must be very slim somewhere. Could you not break him?"

Letter to General Hooker, June 5, 1863: "In one word, I would not take any risk of being entangled upon the river, like an ox jumped half over a fence and liable to be torn by dogs front and rear, without a fair chance to gore one way or kick the other."

THE COMMANDER-IN-CHIEF

After the battle of Gettysburg Lincoln urged Meade in a peremptory order to pursue Lee in his retreat, attack him, and with one bold stroke end the war. A friendly note came with it:

"The order I inclose is not of record. If you succeed, you need not publish the order. If you fail, publish it. Then, if you succeed, you will have all the credit of the movement. If not, I'll take all the responsibility."

Is there in our history a more generous act, a nobler patriotism?

Some question has arisen as to Mr. Lincoln's religious opinions, but this story illustrates his attitude toward religion. A Southern woman who had come to see Lincoln about her husband, who was confined in a Northern prison because of his "pernicious politics," mentioned the fact that the prisoner was a religious man.

"I'm glad to hear that," said Mr. Lincoln, cheerfully; and the lady smiled hopefully in response. Then he went on, "Because any man who wants to disrupt this Union needs all the religion in sight to save him."

Mr. Lincoln's love for the soldiers was well known, and he was a frequent visitor at the hospitals in Washington. A young doctor was showing him around one afternoon to let him speak to the men. The guide took him past the entrance to a large room, saying that he didn't suppose the President wanted to go in there, as they were "only rebels."

"But I do want to go in there," said Lincoln, "and don't you call them 'rebels'; call them 'Johnnies.' It sounds friendlier. Would you want to be called a 'Yank' and neglected because you did the best you knew?"

It is doubtful whether in all history or in all literature there may be found a tribute at once so touching, so comprehensive, and so happy in expression as this. Its brevity and its depth, its sincerity of tone, its poetic beauty, make Lincoln one of the master writers of epistolary literature:

"Dear Madam,—I have been shown, in the files of the War Department, a statement of the Adjutant-General of Massachusetts, that you are the mother of five sons who have died gloriously on the field of battle.

"I feel how weak and fruitless must be any words of mine which should attempt to beguile you from a loss so overwhelming. But I cannot refrain from tendering to you the consolation that may be found in the thanks of the Republic they died to save.

THE COMMANDER-IN-CHIEF

"I pray that our Heavenly Father may assuage the anguish of your bereavement, and leave you only the cherished memory of the loved and lost, and the solemn pride that must be yours to have laid so costly a sacrifice upon the altar of freedom.

"Yours, very sincerely and respectfully,
"ABRAHAM LINCOLN.
"To Mrs. Bixby, Boston, Mass."

In reply to a committee that came to protest about the conduct of the war and to suggest changes, Lincoln told the following anecdote:
"Three moves, it is said, are worse than a fire. There was a family in western Pennsylvania who started their migrations pretty well off in a worldly way. But they moved and moved, having less every time they moved, till after a while they could carry everything in one wagon. It was said that the chickens of the family got so used to being moved that whenever they saw the wagon-sheets brought out they laid themselves on their backs and crossed their legs ready to be tied."

Lincoln's remarkable facility, amounting to genius, for saying things briefly yet with wonderful appositeness is illustrated in the following letter written to Carl Schurz. It contains a world of humor, and yet tells its own story in its own remarkable and peculiar way. Schurz at that time took issue with the Administration as to its policy, and the following letter is a reply to his strictures:

"You think I could do better; therefore, you blame me already. I think I could not do better; therefore, I blame you for blaming me. I understand you now to be willing to accept the help of men who are not Republicans, provided they have 'heart in it.' Agreed. I want no others. But who is to be the judge of hearts or of 'hearts in it'? If I must discard my own judgment and take yours I must also take that of others; and by the time I should reject all I should be advised to reject, I should have none left, Republicans or others—not even yourself. For be assured, my dear sir, there are men who have 'heart in it' that think you are performing your part as poorly as you think I am performing mine."

At the White House one day some gentlemen from the West were much excited and troubled about the commissions or omissions of the Administration. The President heard them patiently, and then replied: "Gentlemen, suppose all the property you were worth was in gold, and

THE COMMANDER-IN-CHIEF

you had put it in the hands of Blondin to carry across the Niagara River on a rope, would you shake the cable, or keep shouting out to him, 'Blondin, stand up a little straighter—Blondin, stoop a little more—go a little faster—lean a little more to the north—lean a little more to the south'? No! You would hold your breath as well as your tongue, and keep your hands off until he was safe over. The Government is carrying an immense weight. Untold treasures are in their hands. They are doing the very best they can. Don't badger them. Keep silence, and we'll get you safe across."

Lincoln frequently showed that he could easily avoid a direct answer and evade inquisitive visitors when he thought it was impolitic to make known his opinions. One of the latter wanted to know his opinion of Sheridan, who had just come from the West to take command of the cavalry under Grant. Said Lincoln:

"I will tell you just what kind of a chap he is. He is one of those long-armed fellows with short legs that can scratch his shins without having to stoop over to do so."

One day, when the vain boasting of a certain general was the subject of discussion, Lincoln was "reminded" of a farmer out in Illinois who was in the habit of bragging about everything he did and had and saw, and particularly about his crops. While driving along the road during the haying season he noticed one of his neighbors hauling a load of hay into his barn. He could not resist the opportunity, and commenced to brag about the size of his hay crop, which, as usual, he asserted to be larger and better than any ever before known in the county. After he had finished he asked what kind of a crop his neighbor had put in.

"The biggest crop you ever see!" was the prompt reply. "I've got so much hay I don't know what to do with it. I've piled up all I can outdoors, and am going to put the rest of it in the barn."

A gentleman asked Lincoln to give him a pass through the Federal lines in order to visit Richmond. "I should be very happy to oblige you," said the President, "if my passes were respected; but the fact is, within the past two years I have given passes to Richmond to two hundred and fifty thousand men, and not one has got there yet."

When the Sherman expedition which captured Port Royal went out, there was a great curiosity

THE COMMANDER-IN-CHIEF

to know where it had gone. A person with ungovernable curiosity asked the President the destination.

"Will you keep it entirely secret?" asked the President.

"Oh yes, upon my honor."

"Well," said the President, "I will tell you." Assuming an air of great mystery and drawing the man close to him, he kept him awaiting the revelation with great anxiety, and then said in a loud whisper, which was heard all over the room, "The expedition has gone to—sea."

An amusing yet touching instance of the President's preoccupation of mind occurred at one of his levees, when he was shaking hands with a host of visitors passing him in a continuous stream. An intimate acquaintance received the usual conventional handshake and salutation, but, perceiving that he was not recognized, kept his ground, instead of moving on, and spoke again; then the President, roused by dim consciousness that something unusual had happened, perceived who stood before him, and, seizing his friend's hand, shook it again heartily, saying, "How do you do? Excuse me for not noticing you at first; the fact is, I was thinking of a man down South." He afterward privately

LINCOLN'S OWN STORIES

acknowledged that the "man down South" was Sherman, then on his march to the sea.

The President at one time received a report that one of our Northern friends had been caught by the rebels in Virginia and condemned to death, the choice being left to him to be hanged or shot. The writer, who was present when this report was made, says that a trace of humor passed over Lincoln's sad face when he said he was reminded of a camp-meeting of old colored Methodists in his earlier days. There was a brother who responded often and with much enthusiasm to the preacher with "Amen" and "Bless de Lawd," etc. The preacher drew a strong line, sweeping the sinners on both sides into the devil's net: "All those who thus sin are in the downward path to ruin, and all those who so act, including the whole human race, are on the sure road to hell." The unctuous brother, bewildered, cried out, "Bless de Lawd, dis nigga takes to de woods."

He was a keen and inveterate foe of all kinds of sham, snobbery, cant, and officialism.

Col. Silas W. Burt and several military friends called on President Lincoln on business for Governor Seymour of New York, late one evening in the summer of '63. As they were about to leave, one of the men, a certain major, under

THE COMMANDER-IN-CHIEF

the influence of liquor, leered at Mr. Lincoln and, slapping him on the leg, said:

"Mr. President, tell us one of your *good* stories"—with significant emphasis on the "good." Colonel Burt thus refers to his mortification:

"If the floor had opened and dropped me out of sight I should have been happy. The President drew himself up, and, turning his back as far as possible upon the major, with great dignity addressed the rest of us, saying:

"'I believe I have the popular reputation of being a story-teller, but I do not deserve the name in its general sense, for it is not the story itself, but its purpose or effect that interests me. I often avoid a long and useless discussion by others, or a laborious explanation on my own part, by a short story that illustrates my point of view. So, too, the sharpness of a refusal or the edge of a rebuke may be blunted by an appropriate story so as to save wounded feelings and yet serve the purpose. No, I am not simply a story-teller, but story-telling as an emollient saves me much friction and distress.'"

In 1863 a certain captain of volunteers was on trial in Washington for a misuse of the funds of his company. The accused officer made only a feeble defense, and seemed to treat the matter with indifference. After a while, however, a new charge, that of disloyalty to the Government, came into the case. The accused was at once excited to a high degree of indignation, and made a very vigorous defense. He appeared to think lightly of being convicted of embezzling, but to be called a traitor was more than he could bear. At the breakfast-table, one morning, the President, who had been reading an account of this case in the newspaper, began to laugh, and said: "This fellow reminds me of a juror in a case of hen-stealing which I tried in Illinois many years ago. The accused man was summarily convicted. After adjournment of court, as I was riding to the next town, one of the jurors in the case came cantering up behind me and complimented me on the vigor with which I had pressed the prosecution of the unfortunate hen-thief. Then he added, 'Why, when I was young, and my back was strong, and the country was new, I didn't mind taking off a sheep now and then. But stealing hens! Oh, Jerusalem!' Now, this captain has evidently been stealing sheep, and that is as much as he can bear."

Charles A. Dana, in his volume of recollections gives a rather interesting incident illustrating Lincoln's remarkable shrewdness:

THE COMMANDER-IN-CHIEF

"A spy whom we employed to report to us the proceedings of the Confederate Government and its agents, and who passed continually between Richmond and St. Catherines, reporting at the War Department upon the way, had come in from Canada and had put into my hands an important despatch from Clement C. Clay, Jr., addressed to Mr. Benjamin. Of course, the seal was broken and the paper read immediately. It showed unequivocally that the Confederate agents in Canada were making use of that country as a starting-point for warlike raids, which were to be directed against frontier towns like St. Albans, in Vermont. Mr. Stanton thought it important that this despatch should be retained as a ground of reclamation to be addressed to the British Government. It was on a Sunday that it arrived, and he was confined to his house by a cold. At his direction I went over to the President and made an appointment with him to be at the Secretary's house after church. At the appointed hour he was there, and I read the despatch to them. Mr. Stanton stated the reasons why it should be retained, and before deciding the question Mr. Lincoln turned to me, saying:

"'Well, Dana?'

"I observed to them that this was a very important channel of communication, and that if we stopped such a despatch as this it was at the risk of never obtaining any more information through that means.

"'Oh,' said the President, 'I think you can manage that. Capture the messenger, take the despatch from him by force, put him in prison, and then let him escape. If he has made Benjamin and Clay believe his lies so far, he won't have any difficulty in telling them new ones that will answer for this case.'

"This direction was obeyed. The paper was sealed up again and was delivered to its bearer. General Augur, who commanded the district, was directed to look for a messenger at such-and-such a place on the road South that evening. The man was brought to the War Department, searched, the paper found upon him and identified, and he was committed to the Old Capitol Prison. He made his escape about a week later, being fired upon by the guard. A large reward for his capture was advertised in various papers East and West, and when he reached St. Catherines with his arm in a sling, wounded by a bullet which had passed through it, his story was believed by Clay and Thompson; or, at any rate, if they had any doubts upon the subject, they were not strong enough to prevent his carrying their messages afterward."

THE COMMANDER-IN-CHIEF

Coming into the President's room one day, Mr. Stanton said that he had received a telegram from General Mitchel, in Alabama, asking instructions. He did not quite understand the situation down there, but, having full confidence in Mitchel's judgment, had answered, "All right; go ahead."

"Now, Mr. President," he added, "if I have made an error, I shall have to get you to countermand the order."

"Once at the cross-roads down in Kentucky, when I was a boy, a particularly fine horse was to be sold," replied Lincoln. "They had a small boy to ride him up and down. One man whispered to the boy as he went by, 'Look here, boy, hain't that horse got splints?' The boy replied, 'Mister, I don't know what splints is; but if it's good for him he's got it, and if it ain't good for him he ain't got it.' Now," added Lincoln, "I understand that if this is good for Mitchel it's all right, but if it's not, I have got to countermand it."

Some enemies and critics of General Grant once called upon Mr. Lincoln and urged him to oust Grant from his command. They repeated with malicious intent the gossip that Grant drank. "What does he drink?" asked Lincoln.

"Whisky," was the answer, "and in unusual quantities." "Well," said the President, "just find out what particular kind he uses, and I'll send a barrel to each of the other generals."

When again pressed on other grounds to get rid of Grant, he declared, "I can't spare that man; he fights."

Wade once came to the President to demand the dismissal of Grant. In reply to one of his remarks Lincoln said, "Senator, that reminds me of a story."

"Yes, yes," Wade replied, "it is with you, sir, all story, story! You are the father of every military blunder that has been made during the war. You are on your road to hell, sir, with this government, by your obstinacy; and you are not a mile off this minute."

Lincoln answered, "Senator, that is just about the distance from here to the Capitol, is it not?" Wade, as Lincoln put it, "grabbed up his hat and cane and went away."

Joseph Medill, editor of the Chicago *Tribune*, told this story to Miss Tarbell. Grant had made a call for 300,000 men, and Lincoln replied that he had already issued a call for 500,000.

THE COMMANDER-IN-CHIEF

"In 1864, when the call for extra troops came, Chicago revolted. She had already sent 22,000 men up to that time, and was drained. When the new call came, there were no young men to go, no aliens except what were bought. The citizens held a mass-meeting, and appointed three persons, of whom I was one, to go to Washington and ask Stanton to give Cook County a new enrolment. I begged off, but the committee insisted, so I went. On reaching Washington, we went to Stanton with our statement. He refused entirely to give us the desired aid. Then we went to Lincoln. 'I cannot do it,' he said, 'but I will go with you to Stanton and hear the arguments of both sides.' So we all went over to the War Department together. Stanton and General Fry were there; and they, of course, contended that the quota should not be changed. The argument went on for some time, and finally was referred to Lincoln, who had been sitting silent, listening. I shall never forget how he suddenly lifted his head and turned on us a black and frowning face.

"'Gentlemen,' he said, in a voice full of bitterness, 'after Boston, Chicago has been the chief instrument in bringing this war on the country. The Northwest has opposed the South, as New England has opposed the South. It is you who are largely responsible for making blood flow as it has. You called for war until we had it. You called for emancipation, and I have given it to you. Whatever you have asked for you have had. Now you come here begging to be let off from the call for men which I have made to carry out the war you have demanded. You ought to be ashamed of yourselves. I have a right to expect better things of you. Go home, and raise your 6,000 extra men. And you, Medill, you are acting like a coward. You and your *Tribune* have had more influence than any paper in the Northwest in making this war. You can influence great masses, and yet you cry to be spared at a moment when your cause is suffering. Go home and send us those men.'

"I couldn't say anything. It was the first time I ever was whipped, and I didn't have an answer. We all got up and went out, and when the door closed, one of my colleagues said: 'Well, gentlemen, the old man is right. We ought to be ashamed of ourselves. Let us never say anything about this, but go home and raise the men.' And we did—6,000 men—making 28,000 in the war from a city of 156,000. But there might have been crape on every door almost in Chicago, for every family had lost a son or a husband. I lost two brothers. It was hard for the mothers."

General Fry had been detailed by the War Office to act as escort to the President on his way to Gettysburg, where he delivered his immortal address. He was urged to make haste, as there was but little time left for the train's departure. The President told this story:

"I feel about this as the convict in one of our Illinois towns felt when he was going to the gallows. As he passed along the road in custody of the sheriff the people, eager to see the execution, kept crowding and pushing past him. At last he called out: 'Boys, you needn't be in such a hurry to get ahead. There won't be any fun till I get there.'"

After he had delivered this masterful piece of oratory, which has been compared to the Sermon on the Mount, he turned to Lamon and said: "Lamon, that speech won't scour."

No collection of Lincolniana is really complete without his greatest masterpiece—the famous Gettysburg oration. It is deservedly placed and ranked among the world's most eloquent and most touching orations. Curiously, its great beauty, its masterly construction, its extreme simplicity were first discerned by Englishmen.

"Fourscore and seven years ago our fathers brought forth on this continent a new nation, conceived in liberty, and dedicated to the proposition that all men are created equal. Now we are engaged in a great civil war, testing whether that nation, or any nation so conceived and so dedicated, can long endure. We are met on a great battle-field of that war. We have come to dedicate a portion of that field, as a final resting-place for those who here gave their lives that their nation might live. It is altogether fitting and proper that we should do this. But, in a larger sense, we cannot dedicate, we cannot consecrate, we cannot hallow, this ground. The brave men, living and dead, who struggled here have consecrated it far above our power to add or detract. The world will little note, nor long remember, what we say here, but it can never forget what they did here. It is for us the living, rather, to be dedicated here to the unfinished work which they who fought here have thus far so nobly advanced. It is rather for us to be here dedicated to the great task remaining before us; that from these honored dead we take increased devotion to that cause for which they gave the last full measure of devotion; that we

THE COMMANDER-IN-CHIEF

here highly resolve that these dead shall not have died in vain, that this nation, under God, shall have a new birth of freedom; and that government of the people, by the people, for the people, shall not perish from the earth."

"I wish, Mr. President," said a government official after a disastrous defeat of the Union army, "that I might be a messenger of good news instead of bad. I wish I could tell you how to conquer or to get rid of those rebellious States."

At this President Lincoln looked up, and a smile came across his face as he said: "That reminds me of two boys out in Illinois who took a short cut across an orchard. When they were in the middle of the field they saw a vicious dog bounding toward them. One of the boys was sly enough to climb a tree, but the other ran around the tree, with the dog following. He kept running until, by making smaller circles than it was possible for his pursuer to make, he gained upon the dog sufficiently to grasp his tail. He held on to the tail with a desperate grip until nearly exhausted, when he called to the boy up the tree to come down and help.

" 'What for?' said the boy.

" 'I want you to help me let this dog go.'

"Now," concluded the President, "if I could only let the rebel States go, it would be all right. But I am compelled to hold on to them and make them stay."

But even in the darkest days of the Rebellion he gave himself up to the lighter things, saying, "I laugh because I must not cry; that's all—that's all."

So when Hood's army was destroyed by Thomas in December, 1864, the President told this story:

"A certain rough, rude, and bullying man in our county had a bulldog, which was as rude, rough, and bullying as his master. Dog and man were the terror of the neighborhood. Nobody dared to touch either for fear of the other. But a crafty neighbor laid a plan to dispose of the dog. Seeing Slocum and his dog plodding along the road one day, the dog a little ahead, this neighbor, who was prepared for the occasion, took from his pocket a chunk of meat, in which he had concealed a big charge of powder, to which was fastened a deadwood slow-match. This he lighted and then threw into the road. The dog gave one gulp at it, and the whole thing disappeared down his throat. He trotted on a few steps, when there was a sort of smothered

THE COMMANDER-IN-CHIEF

roar, the dog blew up in fragments, a fore quarter being lodged in a neighboring tree, a hind quarter on the roof of a cabin, and the rest scattered along the dusty road. Slocum came up and viewed the remains. Then, more in sorrow than in anger, he said, 'Bill war a good dawg; but, as a dawg, I reckon his usefulness is over.'" The President added, with a twinkle of his eye, "Hood's army was a good army. We have been very much afraid of it. But, as an army, I reckon its usefulness is gone."

It was in the last days of the great struggle, when the armies of Grant and Lee were in the throes of the final fight for the possession of the Old Dominion that Lincoln watched them from the rear. "How many prisoners?" he asked, eagerly. Every prisoner meant a merciful ending and a saving of life.

On the night of the surrender of Lee at Appomattox Mr. Lincoln was serenaded by many friends and enthusiastic Northerners. He made the usual kindly conciliatory speech, and cordially invited the erring States to come back into the family.

The band played all sorts of patriotic airs—"Columbia, the Gem of the Ocean," "Star-spangled Banner," and others. Mr. Lincoln, looking toward the band-master, suggested:

"Play 'Dixie' now. It's ours."

So throughout his whole career his attitude was generous toward the South.

THE END